the art of handmade bread

DAN LEPARD

MITCHELL BEAZLEY

the art of handmade bread

DAN LEPARD

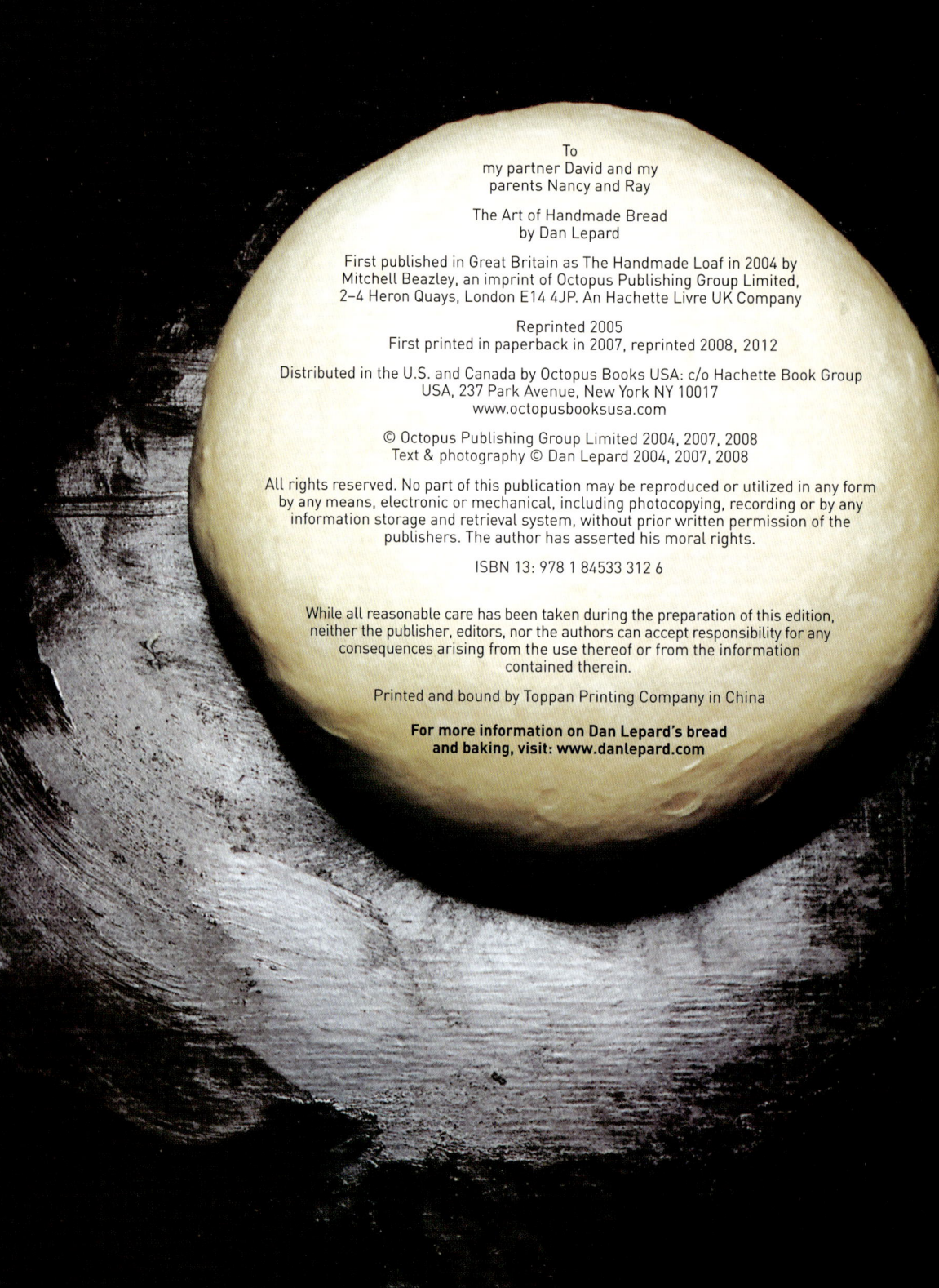

To
my partner David and my
parents Nancy and Ray

The Art of Handmade Bread
by Dan Lepard

First published in Great Britain as The Handmade Loaf in 2004 by
Mitchell Beazley, an imprint of Octopus Publishing Group Limited,
2–4 Heron Quays, London E14 4JP. An Hachette Livre UK Company

Reprinted 2005
First printed in paperback in 2007, reprinted 2008, 2012

Distributed in the U.S. and Canada by Octopus Books USA: c/o Hachette Book Group
USA, 237 Park Avenue, New York NY 10017
www.octopusbooksusa.com

© Octopus Publishing Group Limited 2004, 2007, 2008
Text & photography © Dan Lepard 2004, 2007, 2008

All rights reserved. No part of this publication may be reproduced or utilized in any form
by any means, electronic or mechanical, including photocopying, recording or by any
information storage and retrieval system, without prior written permission of the
publishers. The author has asserted his moral rights.

ISBN 13: 978 1 84533 312 6

While all reasonable care has been taken during the preparation of this edition,
neither the publisher, editors, nor the authors can accept responsibility for any
consequences arising from the use thereof or from the information
contained therein.

Printed and bound by Toppan Printing Company in China

**For more information on Dan Lepard's bread
and baking, visit: www.danlepard.com**

Contents

INTRODUCTION 6

INGREDIENTS 11

MIXING, SHAPING, & BAKING 17

THE NATURAL LEAVEN 23

FROM WATER TO WINE 43

FROM FIELD TO MILL 61

SEEDS AND GRAINS 79

ABUNDANT HARVEST 97

HERBS, SPICES, & FRAGRANCES 121

THE FAT OF THE LAND 143

THE DRY BREADS OF WINTER 165

THE FINISH 186

CONVERSION CHART & ACKNOWLEDGMENTS 190

INDEX 191

Introduction

THE ART OF HANDMADE BREAD is about making the most of what we have; about appreciating what grows in the soil, what is local, and being economical and resourceful with it. We have so much, too much, that we can buy, yet the basic labor of doing, the making with our own hands, is what enlivens us and makes us feel human. Someone once asked me why I bother mixing and shaping bread by hand. I didn't have the words to answer them, nor could I understand why they didn't just know. I will not let my fingers be reduced to simply button-pressing, dial-twirling, or switch-flicking. There is no instrument in my bag of baker's tools more useful and adaptable than my two hands, and as long as I can use them to make and shape bread, I will.

While traveling through northern Europe, I have met people who bake bread in a considered way: bakers who adapt their ingredients according to what is plentiful or scarce at different times of the year. Some bake with wood-fired ovens, some with gas or electric. Some let machines assist them, some bake free-hand. Solitary bakers, and groups of bakers. Many of the recipes that I've written for this book reflect the techniques they use, as well as each baker's response to the ingredients he has at his disposal.

I haven't raided these bakers' personal recipe books, for if I did I couldn't give each community the space it deserves, and nor could I speak their languages well enough to be sure my translations were accurate. But by watching, living, and baking with them, I have distilled the breads we baked into new recipes which walk in the footsteps of those bakers and bring us closer to their traditions. This is the most honest way in which I can convey the breads and methods I encountered, with recipes bakers in other communities can use.

Two steps, though, are significantly different and somewhat heretical. There are no recipes in this book in which the dough is kneaded for 10 minutes on a floured surface, and all the recipes begin with an initial resting period after the ingredients are first combined. After this rest, the dough is kneaded lightly on an oiled surface to combine the ingredients and get the mass even. All the oil does is allow the timid baker to handle sticky dough in a comfortable way, and inhibit the baker from throwing in handfuls of flour in a panic. In time, a scraper and the merest dusting of flour will allow you to achieve the same result. These stages—combined with a gentle manipulation of the dough during an extended rise, giving the yeast time to ferment and aerate—make the soft, sticky dough malleable and easy to shape. All ingredients are weighed, even the water, as this is easy to do with a good set of scales and helps me to translate the handfuls I encountered into something accurate.

The photographs that illustrate the recipes show the actual loaves I baked, made using the instructions given. Most, but not all, were baked (and photographed) in my home, in a gas-fired domestic oven. The temperature dipped up and down during the day, as my neighbors heated their houses or cooked their meals. The thermometer that I hung inside the oven became essential, and told me at what time of the day I was likely to get the oven hot enough, and I'd schedule the baking around that. However, the breads in the

natural leaven chapter were baked and photographed at a restaurant where I work, Locanda Locatelli, the home of the great Italian chef, Giorgio Locatelli. These breads were baked in an electric deck oven, a type some readers will have in their bakeries. The resulting pictures show that the difference between these loaves and the others in the book is not so great, although they are a little better. Good bread is more about dough quality than anything else.

Photographing the book myself was the answer to a problem. So often I have wished for a photographer to be there with me as I baked or worked with other bakers. But budgets don't often stretch to that (bakers are less costly than photographers), and for this book I wanted to show you what I saw, usually with the intimacy that only a solitary traveler can encounter. And the baking clan being what it is, I was accepted as a baker in places where a photographer might have stumbled. The bread was the key, and opened the doors and homes of many extraordinary and talented bakers around Europe. Given the chance, I would write a book about each of them.

In many of the places I visited, home-baking flourished alongside the small independent baker, occasionally in a symbiotic relationship. Bakeries would supply flour, grains, and yeast for home-bakers, and in return the home-bakers would buy bread and sometimes share home-grown ingredients with the bakeries. But always the home-bakers would support the local bakers, buying bread to supplement their effort. I know the effort that goes into a good loaf, and this book doesn't hide the time and thought it takes. So every time I'm in a bakery I remember that, and buy a loaf when I can. If I have too much, then I know I have enough to share.

Ingredients

Cook's notes: weights and measurements

In this book, quantities are given in cups and ounces but also in metric equivalents, an old and easily understandable system of measurement, and one that helps clarify the reasoning behind the recipe. The metric weights given are the most accurate quantities for each recipe. A kilo is a kilo is a kilo wherever you are and that will always hold true, no matter how much kitchen cups and fluid ounces vary. There are imperial fluid ounces and US fluid ounces, Australian cups and US cups, but a gram is the same in Melbourne, Houston, or Edinburgh. Our governments insist we use precisely calibrated weighing systems in commercial transactions, yet there is often no clear way of knowing exactly what the units stand for on domestic measuring jugs, cups, and spoons. Metric measurement also allows for greater precision when translating very personalized recipes. If a baker's recipe is measured in handfuls, I weigh the quantity their hand can hold in grams to get a precise idea of what the weight will be and thus stay true to the recipe. In this book liquid is given in grams so that all ingredients can be weighed together in a single jug or bowl.

Cook's notes: bakers' percentages

Many experienced bakers use a system of measurement based on percentages. If the total weight of flour in a recipe equals 100 percent, then every other ingredient can be described as a percentage of that quantity. These percentages are listed beside the ingredients and are there to help explain the rationale behind the recipe and to enable you to scale up or scale down the recipes as you choose. Please note that the percentages are based on weight, not volume, so cup equivalents can not be used to alter a recipe by this method.

Flour

A bag of flour usually contains milled grain from many different types of wheat. Though some types of wheat are all-round winners, these varieties might also be scarce and/or expensive. A single-grain flour might also be better suited to some purposes than others. By sourcing wheat from different farms, or regions, or even countries, the grain merchant can supply the miller with versatile blends.

This is only possible now that choice is actually available. Immersed in 21st-century retail excess, we can barely imagine a world in which the bulk of the population had no such choice, only what could be grown and delivered locally. But once, all life away from the cities was simple and local. After the Industrial Revolution things started to change, and from the mid-19th century onward the pace of change quickened. Better farming tools, a new chemical industry churning out fertilizers, the scientific analysis of wheat, and the development of faster, more efficient means of transport, all meant that farmers could produce more varieties of grain, in greater volume, and get them to market in the rapidly expanding cities. Ingredients previously scarce or expensive began to be available in larger quantities at an affordable price.

Where a farmer once had a single grain variety, now he had a choice; where a town once had one grain merchant, now there were several. Given this new choice, millers became able to experiment, to produce a single flour with all of the characteristics desirable for breadmaking, and they did this by blending the wheat varieties available. Some varieties helped produce resilient and extensible (stretchy) dough, some a very white or yellow crumb, and some contained high levels of natural sugar in the form of maltose, which gave the finished loaf sweetness and flavor.

Likewise, millers today blend wheat varieties, taking into account the grain color, strength, and flavor, in order to produce flour that will satisfy their baker customers. Though bakers talk of the supreme importance of the gluten quality, the final characteristics of the flour are determined by many factors and may best be judged by both the overall performance of the flour and the specific purpose it will be used for. Don't judge a flour simply by its protein content.

The farmer and miller grade wheat according to the characteristics that not only identify the variety, but also tell us something of the grain's quality. These characteristics include the color (red, white, or mixed), and the structure (soft, medium, or hard). The term "spring wheat" refers to a variety that is planted in March or April and harvested in July or August of the same year. On an organic farm, spring wheat would yield 3½ metric tons of grain per hectare. The term "winter wheat" refers to a variety that is planted in October or November, germinates over the next few weeks, and is harvested the following year, perhaps 10 or 12 days earlier than the spring variety. A typical winter variety, organically farmed, would yield 6 metric tons of grain per hectare of land; almost double the yield from spring wheat.

As farming is a business, farmers need to maximize their yield from each hectare of land. This means farmers may be less likely to plant spring wheat varieties, which don't bring the same financial return—especially if they are supplying customers who view the flour as a cheap, generic commodity. To encourage and support the farming of rare, local, and lower-yielding crops, such as these spring wheats, we must be prepared to pay more for them.

The recipes in this book call for flour from many different grains, as specified in the introduction to the breads. Not all are available at the supermarket; some need to be searched out or ordered in advance. But without the recipes, there won't be the interest. And without the interest, the grains just won't be grown.

Gluten in flour

Gluten is a complex, sticky, elastic protein that is present in the flour from many grains. In wheat flour it is the gluten that traps the carbon dioxide released by the yeasts as they ferment the sugars in the dough, creating a bold, well-risen loaf, and it is the gluten that provides the skeletal structure in the crumb. In rye flour, it is proteins similar to gluten that give the dough its stickiness, but without the elasticity or extensibility of wheat dough.

The protein content listed in the nutritional information on the side of a bag of flour will not tell you the gluten content. The gluten in wheat flour only accounts for up to 80 percent of the total protein. The other 20 percent or so is made up mostly of soluble protein, which will thicken when salt is added or when it is baked, adding to the texture of the finished loaf. A small percentage of the protein is insoluble, forming part of the grain structure. But it is the gluten which, when hydrated, forms a complex structure bound together with very small quantities of carbohydrates, fats, and minerals present in the flour.

The gluten is best seen as a continuous network within the dough, which binds lipids (fats) and entraps starch. For this reason, bread has been described as "gluten foam." The gluten itself has no flavor or aroma; these are carried by the starches and lipids in the flour. The recognizable flavor of good bread is created when these starches and fats are combined with bacteria and enzymes found naturally in the flour, or introduced by the yeast or ferment.

The two main constituents of gluten are: gliadin, a sticky substance that helps to bind the gluten into a cohesive compound and contributes to the viscosity and stretchiness of the dough; and glutenin, which gives the dough its strength and resilience. It is variations in the characteristics of the glutenin that account for most of the differences between types of wheat flours. Two flours can have a similar protein content, yet behave vastly differently. Experiment, talk to your miller, and find out which flours you prefer.

Yeast

FRESH YEAST VERSUS ACTIVE DRY YEAST Yeast belongs to the family of organisms known as fungi. When added to a mixture of water and flour, it will use the sugars contained in the flour in order to ferment, releasing carbon dioxide as it does so. This aerates the mixture. When baked, the yeast is killed, but the aeration in the dough remains, giving a light texture to the loaf. The yeast you buy has been grown selectively in order to supply the baker with a pure strain that will multiply quickly at a predictable rate and aerate the dough adequately.

I've found a marked improvement in the results I achieve when baking with fresh yeast. To replicate the results in this book, I would recommend that you seek out and use fresh yeast where required. However, in many instances this is difficult, usually because the demand isn't there to warrant local availability. In many northern European countries, small blocks of fresh yeast weighing 50g are widely available in small supermarkets. This is because more people bake at home in these countries, in addition to supporting their local bakery. If we start to bake more at home, we can demand the same convenience.

When you need to replace the fresh yeast in the recipe with active dry yeast, do the following. Take 25 percent of the water from a recipe and heat it to 100–104°F. Whisk in the dry yeast (half the weight given for fresh yeast), together with 2–3 tbsp of flour from the total amount. Leave this for 20 minutes, then use in the recipe as if using fresh yeast.

NATURAL LEAVEN VERSUS COMMERCIAL YEAST Prior to the widespread availability of commercially prepared yeast, bakers would leave a mixture of flour and water to ferment, and use this as the source of yeast for their recipe. The yeasts that naturally collect on surfaces and grains multiply more slowly than the commercial strains, produce less carbon dioxide, and prefer cooler temperatures. This method is increasingly practiced by bakers who want to re-establish old flavors and textures by using techniques shaped over hundreds of years. By doing so they are creating breads that sell very well to a public increasingly disenchanted with the bland taste of mass-market foods.

The adage here must be to bake with what you have; make the best of what is around you. For some, there is no choice in their minds but to use a natural leaven as the sole ferment within a dough. For others, this is akin to witchcraft, and a madness in an age of convenience. To my mind, a beautiful loaf, wrought with care and consideration, must be the aim; and in trying to write a useful book, I have come to understand that for each reader this means something different. How you get to the end loaf does matter, and the choice you make must be honest and heartfelt. If you have never tried baking with the slower yeasts, then try at least once—or more. Through practice you will begin to understand the simplicity of natural leaven baking, and how its construction, appearance, and aroma will echo through the loaf.

BLOCKS OF FRESH YEAST in the Ukraine, Russia, and Sweden, sold in small 50g units for home use.

Sea salt and malted grains

Sometimes the ingredients we most want to use are not in a form that is best suited to baking. Yet somehow when we are shown them again in a perfect, processed form, they are less alluring. How difficult is it to prepare ingredients ourselves and make them suitable for our needs? Not very, and the results are sometimes preferable.

SALT There is a type of gray sea salt that is available from health-food stores in continental Europe, though less readily available in the US. This salt is one of the things I return with when I travel. It is made up of coarse, hard, roundish crystals that don't dissolve easily in water. If this is not available, look for the purest salt you can find, without anti-caking agents, and go to the bother of grinding it yourself. The best and easiest way is with a large mortar and pestle. Measure out the salt, or weigh in a small cup, then tip this into the mortar and grind it in a circular motion with the pestle.

SALT QUANTITY IN RECIPES My view is that, for the majority of bread recipes, the salt is an integral part of the loaf, and that bread usually needs to be considered a sodium-rich foodstuff, almost like salt-cured fish. Salt is part of the taste and enhances the flavor of the grain. But we eat to live, or should do if we respect the body that carries us, and it is right and proper that we vary our diet according to what our needs are. Please do vary or omit the salt used in the recipes here. We are told that even a small reduction in our dietary sodium intake will benefit us, and many of our processed foods have a hidden sodium (salt) content where you wouldn't expect it to be—in breakfast cereal, for example. For children, two slices of bread can sometimes equal their recommended daily sodium requirement (which is surprisingly small). So use salt respectfully.

MALT Malt occurs naturally in minute amounts in wheat grains. If the grain is left to sprout, enzymes will convert starch into maltose, which will be used by the seedling for growth. If the sprouted grain is dried, gently roasted and ground, the resulting powder can be mixed with the flour to add color and flavor to the final loaf, and will be fermented by the yeast. Throughout Europe, malt has been traditionally and widely used in bread baking, and some old water mills still have a roasting oven for the toasting of sprouted grains. It is, however, in the world of beer and brewing where the full range of malt colors and strengths can be seen. A home-brewing store, if there is one near you, can supply a range of natural malted grains, and these simply require grinding in order to be used; a coffee or spice grinder (the kind of accessory you usually find tucked in the box when you buy a blender) is the perfect tool. Measure out the weight of malt needed, then tip it into the spice or coffee grinder and in seconds it will be reduced to a powder that can be mixed with the flour.

Mixing, shaping, & baking

Mixing the dough

Through necessity and perhaps in an attempt to emulate the gentler mixing of the artisan bakers' preferred twin-arm mixers, I have evolved a hand-kneading method that borders on no-kneading. I haven't invented or discovered anything; as I read and talked with other bakers, I realized that others have also nudged toward a similar conclusion.

For me, it started years ago, when I worked as a pastry chef in a restaurant and had several different bread dough recipes on the go at once. At the same time I was also racing around trying to get ice cream churned, two tarts baked, peaches roasted, and rock-hard pears simmered to tender perfection, while staying calm, organized, and ever-willing to respond with a polite "*Oui*, chef." And yep, I'd forget the bread.

Well, not exactly forget, but I'd get so caught up in other work that I'd start mixing one dough, then leave it for 10–15 minutes while I mixed the next one; then cover and leave that while I raced downstairs to check the ice-cream machine. Then I'd go back upstairs to quickly knead the dough again. And I'd realize that, during the wait, something remarkable had happened to the dough. Within seconds of returning to knead the dough again, it felt smooth and resilient. I'd cover the dough, leave it another 10–15 minutes, race around doing other things, and when I returned and began to knead the dough once more it appeared even smoother and more elastic. It was as if it had been perfectly kneaded for 10 minutes.

Then I tried another variation. Rather than kneading on a flour-dusted work-surface, which always slightly reduced the moisture content of the dough, I tried lightly oiling the work-surface each time. This stopped the dough from sticking, but made certain that the recipe stayed true to the carefully crafted percentages of water-to-flour that gave the loaf its particular crumb structure.

For the last 10 years this has been my preferred method of mixing bread dough in small quantities (under 11lb/5kg). It is better than by machine for small quantities, and great even in small bakeries, when only a few loaves are needed.

PRE-MIXING WITHOUT LEAVENING, AND DELAYING THE ADDITION OF SALT The technique described above had, in fact, been investigated years earlier. In his studies in the early 1970s, the French bakery writer Professor Raymond Calvel found that the full hydration of flour and its gluten occurs over time rather than instantaneously. After mixing flour with water, a short pause of 10–20 minutes allows the particles of flour to swell with moisture, and gives the protein strands of gliadin and glutenin time to hydrate. If the addition of leaven, which is already fully hydrated, is delayed until after this has occurred, the effect on both the dough's resilience, extensibility, and crumb structure is pronounced. If you delay the addition of salt as well, which has a tightening effect on the gluten, then the benefit of this process (known as autolysis) is amplified. For the recipes in this book, I have not delayed the addition of leaven or salt, but once you are comfortable with your technique, then do so.

KNEADING ON AN OILED SURFACE
1 Lightly oil a small, clean patch of work-surface.
2 Scrape the dough out of the bowl and onto the oiled surface.
3 Knead for 5–10 seconds. Stop kneading before the dough absorbs the oil and sticks to the surface.
4 Flip the dough over and leave to rest.

MANIPULATING THE DOUGH DURING THE INITIAL RISE
This is common practice among artisan bakers—it elongates the bubbles formed by the yeast and so changes the dough's handling properties.
1 Stretch the dough out on the work-surface and pat it out lightly into a rectangle.
2 Fold the dough back in on itself by thirds, first in one direction and then in the other.

MIXING DOUGH BY HAND Take the measured amount of liquid and stir into it the yeast or natural leaven, breaking up any lumps. Weigh the dry ingredients. Stir the dry ingredients with the liquid quickly and smoothly. The aim is to try and get the liquid evenly mixed at first, and since the flour will begin to clump as soon as it makes contact with the liquid, the quicker you can mix this the better. Dig your hands right down to the bottom of the bowl to make sure there is neither a clump of flour nor a pool of liquid sitting there. Then squidge the dough through the fingers of your hand so that there are few lumps left. Scrape whatever dough is sticking to your hands back into the bowl, then cover the dough and leave for 10 minutes (or whatever time is suggested in the recipe).

Lightly oil a small, clean patch of work-surface. Scrape the dough from the bowl out onto the oiled surface and knead briefly for 5–10 seconds, stopping before the dough absorbs the oil and sticks. Cover the dough with a cloth, and quickly clean the bowl out with warm water (this will help keep the dough free from stray bits that could harden on the inner surface of the bowl). Dry and lightly oil the bowl, then lift the dough from the work-surface and replace it in the bowl. Cover with a cloth and leave for 10 minutes (or whatever time is suggested in the recipe).

Each time you knead the dough, it should be a conscious and deliberate act rather than a frantic aerobic activity. Initially you are looking to mix the moisture through the dough evenly, watching out for any lumps that need breaking with your fingers and combining the ingredients into one smooth, uniform, and cohesive mass.

Now repeat the kneading once more. Spread a little more oil on the work-surface, then remove the dough from the bowl and begin to knead it gently once more, for 10–15 seconds. You will notice at once that the dough seems smoother and more resilient. Also, as the yeast cells release carbon dioxide into the dough, these bubbles will become stretched and elongated during the repeated kneading, which will result in the crumb of the loaf having an open texture.

TURNING THE DOUGH It has become common for artisan bakers, both in commercial bakeries and at home, to manipulate the dough during the initial rise. This involves stretching the dough out on the work-surface, patting it out lightly into a rectangle, then folding it back in on itself by thirds, first in one direction and then the other. This gentle stretching elongates the bubbles formed by the fermenting yeast and in doing so changes the handling properties of dough with a high (68 percent plus) water content. Much like the strength that is created in a cellular foam such as a whipped meringue, the surface tension that each bubble creates helps the dough to sit upright rather than spread in a flowing mass on the bench.

If I'm making a dough with a high percentage of water, I first place it in an oiled and lipped tray that is large enough to cope with the inevitable flow of the dough. Then, as the dough is gently stretched and folded during the initial fermentation, it appears to gain resilience as the texture becomes more open. By the end, and before its final weighing and shaping, this liquid dough has transformed into a manageable and workable mass.

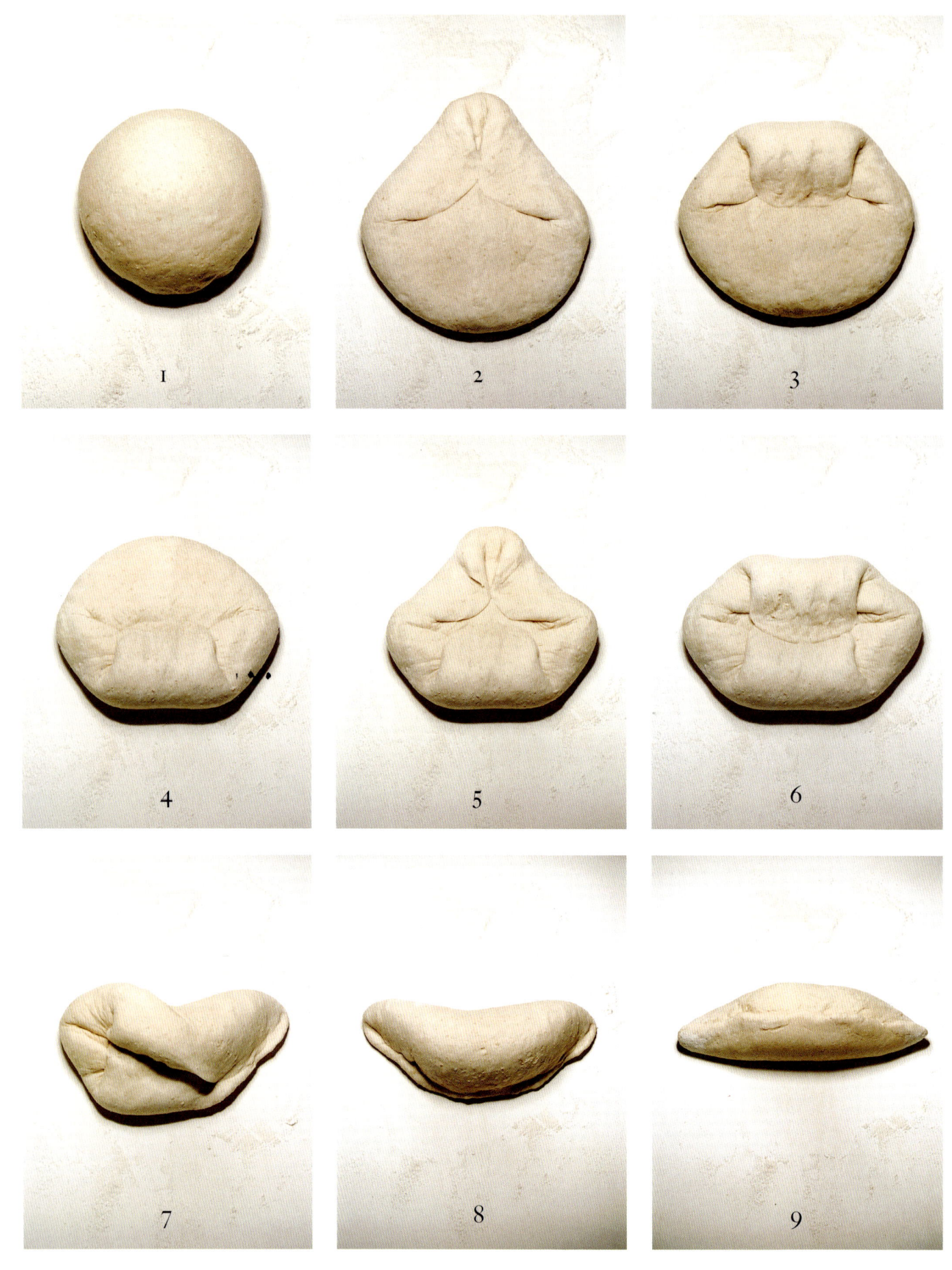

Shaping the dough

SHAPING A BATON (1) Shape the dough into a ball, cover and allow to rest for 10 minutes. This gets the dough into a neat, even shape first, and helps to ensure that the final oval shape is symmetrical.
(2) Pat the dough out into a flat oval, seam-side-up. Imagine the piece of dough has four curved sides. Take the two sides furthest from you and fold them in to the center, pressing them down well so that they seal.
(3) Then take the point that has formed and fold that in to the center, pressing it down to seal it well.
(4) Next, flip the dough around 180°.
(5/6) Repeat with the other side. This flipping helps to keep the dough shape even. Then flip the dough around once more.
(7) Fold the dough evenly in half toward you.
(8) Seal both edges together with the heel of your hand.
(9) Roll the dough back and forward on the work-surface, pressing down ever so slightly with your hands so that any trapped air in the folded shape is forced out toward the ends. If you increase the pressure placed by the outer part of both hands, you can give the loaf pointed ends. Place the dough seam-side-up on a floured cloth.

SHAPING A BALL Place the piece of dough, with the smoothest side facing downward, onto the oiled or lightly floured surface. With your right hand (if you are right-handed), start folding the edges of the piece of dough in toward the center, then hold each in place with the thumb of the left hand while you rotate the dough and fold again eight times, creating a roughly octagonal piece of dough with all of the edges pinched in toward the center. Now flip the dough over. Without too much flour or oil on the surface, drag the dough from left to right (if you are right-handed), rotating it clockwise but forcing it to stick ever so slightly to the work-surface.

Think about this. What is happening is that the slight adhesion of the dough to the work-surface pulls the outer surface of the dough. Then, as you are also pushing and slowly rotating the dough across the work-surface, this causes the outer surface of the dough to be pulled very tight. This is exactly what you want. No more spinning the dough on a heavily floured surface; let it stick just slightly as you push and rotate it gently so that the outer surface becomes taut and smooth. Do this two or three times, but no more as the dough would then start to tear. Place the dough seam-side-up on a floured cloth.

SHAPING A STICK Initially shape the dough into a baton (as above), cover and then allow to rest for 10 minutes. Starting at one end, fold the dough in half once more while at the same time sealing the edges together with the heel of your hand. Finally, roll the dough back and forward on the work-surface, pressing down ever so slightly with your hands so that any trapped air in the folded shape is forced out toward the ends and the dough is gradually stretched into a long stick. If you increase the pressure placed by the outer part of both hands, you can give the stick pointed ends. Place the dough seam-side-up on a floured cloth.

Slashing the dough

In theory, you could ensure that your loaf rises to its fullest extent prior to baking. Then it would only expand a little in the oven and achieve a perfect, unbroken crust. But in reality this is not only difficult to achieve but also undesirable because, should there be an unexpected delay the moment before your loaf goes into the oven, the whole baking session could be ruined as a result. Don't take this risk.

Instead, bakers have turned this problem into a beautiful tradition. If the loaf goes into the oven with a cut across the surface before the dough has fully expanded (or when the dough is "young"), then it will rise and tear along that cut. This deliberate slicing through the skin of the dough ensures that expansion will break through where the least surface tension exists.

To slash the dough, get a very sharp blade from a craft store (or use a safety razor blade). Being especially careful not to cut yourself, hold the blade at an angle, and with a swift action slash the surface of the dough. If this troubles you, then you can also clip at the surface of the dough with a pair of scissors.

Baking the loaf

It is worth investing in a few pieces of equipment. First, get an oven thermometer. Just before starting this book I checked my oven at home. The dial said 425°F; the thermometer said 350°F. Bread will still bake adequately in a lower temperature oven, but it will take longer to get a good crust, bake paler and look less dramatic. If your oven cannot reach 425°F, just increase the baking time.

Modern domestic ovens are designed to do best what we do most often: reheat food. They're not really designed for baking, but aim to keep food dry and crisp, which is just what we don't want. An Aga is an exception, as it doesn't let much moisture escape during baking. Great for us bakers (not so good for ready-meal peddlers). For the first 10 minutes of baking, the loaf needs to expand to its fullest extent and its surface needs to stay soft and supple in order to do this. A moist environment enables this to happen. To overcome the dryness of modern ovens, invest in a refillable fine-misting water spray. A quick spray onto the cut surface of the dough just before it goes into the oven, and again after 5 minutes, seems to help produce a dramatic tear in the loaf. This can be done in addition to ice cubes tossed into a hot baking sheet, or water sprayed inside the oven just before the bread goes in.

If you are using a baking stone, place that in the oven and allow it to heat up before baking. This helps retain the heat in the oven, which is useful if you have one of these modern domestic ovens that is woefully lacking in insulation and works somewhat better as a kitchen heater. A hot, thick metal tray will also act as a baking surface. Most of the recipes in this book assume the reader wants to place the bread on a cold tray or baking sheet and then place that in the hot oven. A better result will be achieved if you upturn the loaf onto a thin semolina-dusted board (what bakers call a peel or a pizza shovel), and then deposit the loaf onto the hot stone or tray. When cold dough is placed on a hot stone, there is a sudden outward push from the steam created inside the dough, which improves both the loaf's internal texture and boldness. It is only recently that research groups worldwide, through the use of the latest scientific measurements, are beginning to understand this ancient process; for example, by the thermal imaging of baking loaves done by Professor Laurie Hall at Cambridge University.

The natural leaven

Creating a leaven

Leavened bread is bread that has risen, puffed with gases that create a cellular network of pockets throughout the dough. These gases are produced by fermentation, a process whereby an organism, in this case one of the Saccharomyces strain of fungi we know as "yeast," releases carbon dioxide as it assimilates and uses the sugars present in the dough. Bacteria can also ferment sugars, and are often present together with yeast when fermentation occurs.

Yeast might be found on the surface of grains such as wheat, or on the skin of fruits rich in sugars, or in a spoonful of an already fermenting mixture. When these are mixed with fresh water and flour, the yeasts will slowly multiply and ferment. Some bacteria will give the leaven its distinctive sour aroma and taste—as with the bacterium Lactobacillus Sanfrancisco, which has been isolated by scientists, and to which the remarkable bright flavor of the San Francisco sourdough is attributed.

A simple mixture of flour and water, stirred and left in a warm place, may ferment and produce an active leaven. In Sweden, I mixed locally milled rye flour with water, and refreshed it with additional flour and water daily. By day five, it was bubbling with fermentation and the actual leaven is shown in the picture below. But I haven't always been so lucky. The recipe that I have relied on in the past, which is shown on the following pages, contains two other ingredients: raisins, since it is likely that they will harbor yeast on their surface; and yogurt, because it contains lactic bacteria. All the breads using leaven in this book have been made with a leaven initiated from this recipe.

This recipe, as well as samples of the leaven it produces, was sent to the National Collection of Yeast Cultures (NCYC) in Norwich, UK. They followed the recipe, and by day five the fermentation had begun. But we were curious about exactly which organisms had caused it. So the ingredients were streaked out on standard YM agar plates to look for yeast or bacterial colonies. After one week at 77°F the sample from the raisins produced the largest amount of yeast, with a small amount also being found in the wheat flour. The yogurt, and to a much lesser extent the rye flour, produced only bacterial colonies. It is speculated that these bacteria multiply in the initial mixture and alter it by breaking down the flour and lowering the pH until the yeast gradually multiply and take over. A leaven given to me in Denmark by Eva Hauch (see page 72), and reputed by Eva to be more than 100 years old, was also tested. This contained many different yeast and bacterial cells. It is possible that leaven might develop a complex variety of yeast and bacterial cultures according to what it is refreshed with over a long period of time.

The yeasts in your leaven will initially multiply very slowly. By adding fresh water and flour to the leaven once or twice a day, the chances of a strong and healthy fermentation are increased. Ideally, after the sixth day onward, each new addition (or "refreshment") should be four or five times the quantity that is in the jar. Do this, and the yeasts in the leaven will multiply at an optimum rate in the reduced pH, will stay healthy, and will produce enough carbon dioxide to aerate your bread successfully.

Leaven recipe

Here is a recipe, or perhaps more correctly a set of ingredients and steps, that will promote fermentation in a leaven of flour and water. Though fermentation will occur simply with flour and water, I have added a few other ingredients that I like and have grown accustomed to. (I have also tried making the leaven solely with organic rye flour, using slightly less than the suggested amount of white flour; it worked a treat.) I photographed every step of making the leaven each morning in my home kitchen so that you can see exactly what the process should look like.

DAY 1

3 tbsp (50g) water at 68°F
2 rounded tsp rye flour
2 rounded tsp bread flour
2 rounded tsp currants or raisins
2 rounded tsp live low-fat yogurt

Mix all the ingredients in a 2-cup Kilner jar. Cover and leave at room temperature (approx. 68°F) for 24 hours.

DAY 2

3 tbsp (50g) water at 68°F
2 rounded tsp rye flour
2 rounded tsp bread flour

By this stage there will be no perceptible change, though some yeasts will have multiplied. The surface will look shiny as the solids separate from the water and sink down in the jar. Stir the above ingredients into the leaven, starting with the water, followed by the dry ingredients. Cover and leave again at room temperature (approx. 68°F) for 24 hours.

DAY 3

6 tbsp (100g) water at 68°F
4 rounded tsp bread flour
4 rounded tsp rye flour

By this time the raisins (or currants) will have started to break down and you will notice a coffee-colored ring around them as they sit in the mixture. Also, there will be the odd pin hole of fermentation on the surface. Add the water, stir well to combine, then add the flours and stir again. The mixture will look frothy, but this is simply from the stirring. Nearly there. Cover and leave again at room temperature (approx. 68°F) for 24 hours.

DAY 4

6 tbsp (100g) water at 68°F
1 scant cup (125g) bread flour

By this time the froth of fermentation should be beginning, though there will be only the vaguest hint of acidity in the aroma. Remove and discard three-quarters of the mixture. Add the water and stir well. Pour the mixture through a tea strainer to remove the raisins (or currants), then put the strained liquid back into the Kilner jar. Add the flour and stir again. Cover and leave at room temperature (approx. 68°F) for 24 hours.

DAY 5

6 tbsp (100g) water at 68°F
1 scant cup (125g) bread flour

The fermentation should be clearly evident, and the aroma starting to become acid. You can notice this the moment you remove the lid from the jar, though it disappears quickly. Remove and discard three-quarters of the mixture. Add the water and stir well so that the mixture thins evenly. Stir in the flour so that you have a thick paste. I prefer to keep the refreshment slightly heavier on flour than water, as this slows the fermentation and stops the leaven rising and falling too quickly. Cover and leave again at room temperature (approx. 68°F) for 24 hours.

DAY 6 ONWARD Take the lid off the jar, and you will see the mixture bubbling. Each day, as you remove some leaven for baking, replacing it with an equivalent amount of flour and water, the aroma of the leaven will become stronger and more sharply acidic.

THE NATURAL LEAVEN | LEAVEN RECIPE

DAY 1 Mix water, flour, raisins, and yogurt together in the proportions stated in the recipe on page 25, in a small Kilner jar and leave at room temperature for 24 hours.

DAY 2 The surface should look shiny. Add water and flour in the proportions stated in the recipe on page 25, and again leave at room temperature for 24 hours.

DAY 3 The raisins will have started to break down. Again add water and flour in the proportions stated in the recipe on page 25, and leave at room temperature for 24 hours.

DAY 4 By now the froth of fermentation should be beginning. Again add water and flour in the proportions stated in the recipe on page 25, pour the mixture through a strainer, and return the strained liquid to the jar. Leave for 24 hours.

DAY 5 By now the fermentation should be clearly evident and the aroma acidic. Discard three-quarters of the mixture. Add water in the proportions stated in the recipe on page 25, stir, then add and stir in flour. Leave for another 24 hours.

TO STORE THE LEAVEN FOR USE If used regularly, some bakers keep their leaven at room (or bakery) temperature, others keep it chilled at 54–59°F. Regular refreshment, for at least two days prior to baking, is needed to keep the leaven active and in prime condition.

TO STORE THE LEAVEN FOR USE ANOTHER TIME If you want to store the leaven, without using it, for longer periods, this will force some of the yeast cells to become dormant and some to die. Leave the leaven covered and undisturbed at the back of the refrigerator (at 39°F). As it sits unrefreshed, the leaven will separate into a dark coffee-colored liquid, which sits on top, and a solid gray mixture, which lies at the bottom of the jar.

TO REVIVE THE LEAVEN Carefully take 1–2 tsp of the gray putty-like leaven from the bottom of the stored jar, and stir this into a fresh quantity of 6 tbsp (100g) (80%) water and 1 scant cup (125g) (100%) white flour. Leave at room temperature (approx. 68°F) for 24 hours, then remove three-quarters and refresh once more with 6 tbsp (100g) of water and 1 scant cup (125g) white flour. Leave for another 24 hours, by which time the mixture should have fermented again. For the next refreshment, add sufficient fresh flour and water, in proportions by weight of 80% water to 100% flour, to make enough leaven for your baking. Stir well, cover for 24 hours, and use in baking the following day.

ABOVE: DAY 6 Take the lid off the jar and you will see the mixture bubbling. Each day, as you continue to remove leaven for baking, replace it with an equivalent amount of flour and water.
LEFT: The unrefreshed leaven after two months stored in a refrigerator.

White leaven bread

If soda makes a quick bread, then this recipe, using the leaven made on the previous pages, is a very, very slow bread. The yeast you have cultured has multiplied slowly, together with lactic bacteria, to create a distinctive, sour taste to the crumb. The extended kneading during the initial fermentation, or rise, will help to stretch the minute air bubbles released by the yeast, enlarging them to create a web of exaggerated holes throughout the crumb. I've suggested times to help give an indication of how long the process will take, from that first drop of water hitting the flour until the unbaked loaf finally enters the hot oven.

TIP Clear time to make this and the other loaves in this chapter. You can stretch the times by altering the temperatures, for example by mixing the dough at night, leaving it in the refrigerator overnight, removing it in the morning and letting it return to 61–64°F, together with a light kneading (or by turning the dough, see page 19). All breads can only be made if they suit the time you have available, whether in a bakery or in your home.

7oz (200g) white leaven (see pages 25–27) at 64°F (40%)
1⅓ cups (325g) cold water at 61°F (65%)
3 ⅔ cups (500g) bread flour (100%)
1½ tsp fine sea salt (2%)
optional: 1½ tsp ground malted grains (see page 39) (1.5%)
semolina, for dusting the sheet or peel

8.00AM In a large bowl, beat the leaven with the water (and ground malted grains, if using). Add the flour and salt, and stir together with your hands until you have a soft, sticky mass. The dough temperature should be about 68°F. Scrape any remaining dough from your hands, cover the bowl and leave for 10 minutes. Wash and dry your hands, removing stuck bits of dough from your fingers.

8.10AM Remove the dough from the bowl and place on a lightly oiled (with corn or olive oil) or flour-dusted work-surface. Knead the dough for 10–15 seconds. While this initially seems a short knead, it is still important to work the dough thoroughly. I find by kneading the dough 12 times, rotating it in quarter turns, this can be achieved. Shape the dough into a ball, and leave covered on the work-surface. Clean and dry the bowl, and give it a light rub inside with oil.

8.20AM Knead the dough for 10–15 seconds, shape into a ball, and then place the dough back in the bowl. Cover and leave at room temperature (68°F) for 10 minutes.

8.30AM Knead the dough for 10–15 seconds, shape into a ball, and then place the dough back in the bowl. Cover and leave for 30 minutes.

9.00AM Knead the dough for 10–15 seconds, shape into a ball, and then place the dough back in the bowl. Cover and leave for 1 hour.

10.00AM Knead the dough for 10–15 seconds, shape into a ball, and then place the dough back in the bowl. Cover and leave for 1 hour.

11.00AM Knead the dough for 10–15 seconds, shape into a ball, and then place the dough back in the bowl. Cover and leave for 2 hours.

1.00PM Divide the dough into two pieces, each roughly 1lb 2oz (500g) in weight. Shape each piece into a ball, cover, and leave on the work-surface for 15 minutes.

1.15PM Rub two clean dishtowels with flour, then use them to line two bowls (8in wide), or use flour-dusted, linen-lined baskets if you have them (though expensive, they last a long time). Dust the work-surface with flour. Shape the dough once more into balls, and then place each seam-side-up in the flour-dusted cloths sitting inside the bowls. Cover the upper surface with a cloth, and leave at room temperature (68°F) until almost doubled in height—around 4½ hours.

5.30PM Preheat the oven to 425°F. As naturally leavened loaves rise much more slowly, there isn't the same urgency when it comes to time to bake the loaf. Dust a baking sheet, or a peel if you are using an oven stone, with semolina. Upturn one loaf onto the sheet (or peel), and with a sharp blade cut a circle around the circumference of the loaf. Spray the top of the loaf with water, and bake for 50–70 minutes. Cool on a wire rack. Bake the remaining loaf using the same technique.

The mill loaf

This loaf uses a mix of white, wholewheat, and rye flour, and this recipe could make use of any other grain flours (60% white to 40% other flour) so long as the white flour stays dominant. The method is almost identical to the white leaven bread on page 28, but the result is quite different, with a dark, nutty, sour taste to the crust and crumb.

1lb 2oz (500g) white leaven (50%) (see pages 25–27)
2¼ cups (550g) water at 68°F (55%)
optional: 1 tsp ground malted grains (0.5%) (see page 39)
4⅕ cups (600g) bread flour (60%)
2½ cups (300g) whole-wheat flour (30%)
1 scant cup (100g) rye flour (10%)
2½ tsp fine sea salt (2%)

8.00AM In a large bowl, beat the leaven with the water (and malt, if using). Add the flours and salt, and stir with your hands until you have a soft, sticky mass. The dough temperature should be about 68°F. Scrape any dough from your hands, cover the bowl, and leave for 10 minutes. Wash and dry your hands and any utensils.

8.10AM Remove the dough from the bowl and place on a lightly oiled (with corn or olive oil) or flour-dusted work-surface. Knead the dough for 10–15 seconds, or 12 times, rotating it in quarter turns. Shape the dough into a ball, and leave covered on the work-surface for 10 minutes. Clean the bowl, and give it a light rub with oil.

8.20AM Knead the dough for 10–15 seconds, shape into a ball, then place back in the bowl. Cover and leave at room temperature (about 68°F) for a 10 minutes.

8.30AM Knead the dough for 10–15 seconds, shape into a ball, then place back in the bowl. Cover and leave for 30 minutes.

9.00AM Knead the dough for 10–15 seconds, shape into a ball, then place back in the bowl. Cover and leave for 1 hour.

10.00AM Knead the dough for 10–15 seconds, shape into a ball, then place back in the bowl. Cover and leave for 1 hour.

11.00AM Dust the work-surface with flour. Divide the dough into two equal pieces. Gently knead each piece for 10 seconds and round into a ball. Cover and leave for 10 minutes on the work-surface, to give the dough time to relax. Rub a clean dishtowel with flour, so the dough doesn't stick to it, and lay across a large tray.

11.15AM Sit a ball of dough seam-side-upward on the floured work-surface (see page 20). Pat it flat with your hands, then take the left and right sides furthest from you and fold them in toward the center by ¾in, making a triangular point. Take that point and fold it inward to the center, pressing it down to seal. Rotate the dough 180°, then repeat with the other side. Rotate the dough again, back to the start position.

If you're right-handed, fold the dough in half toward you, starting at the right-hand end, sealing it with the heel of your right hand while holding and folding it with your left. Roll the shaped loaf with both hands, pressing slightly more with the heel of each hand to give the ends a point. Place the dough seam-side-up on the cloth. Fold and pull the cloth up the sides of the loaf (if using a linen-lined basket, just place the dough seam-side upwards inside). Repeat with the remaining dough and sit this next to the first piece, separated by the cloth. Cover with a cloth, and leave at room temperature (68°F) until almost doubled in height—about 4 hours.

3.30–4.30PM Preheat the oven to 425°F. Dust a baking sheet, or a peel if you are using an oven stone, with semolina. Upturn one loaf onto the sheet and cut two slashes across it. Spray the top of the loaf with water and bake for 50–70 minutes. Cool on a wire rack. Bake the remaining loaf using the same technique.

Sour 100% rye bread

This is one of those legendary breads that become easier once you understand the method used. Jan Hedh, the esteemed Swedish baker, who has taught and inspired most of the new breed of artisan bakers in that country and is an inspiration throughout Scandinavia, enlightened me on how to work with and manipulate rye flour. The mixture of almost boiling water with a small amount of rye flour, used as both an addition to the dough and a wash over the exterior of the loaf, gives elasticity to both the crust and crumb. As it was traditional in rural societies to cook grains as a mash with water, you can imagine leftovers finding their way into the baker's mix.

TIP For the gelatinized mixture, it is worth noting that different temperatures of hot water produce different results. Try two different mixes, one with the water at 194°F and one with the water at 176°F, and see which you prefer. Use fine rye flour or, if you have trouble finding it, sift coarse rye flour and save the rye bran for dressing the loaf or dusting your rising baskets.

FOR THE GELATINIZED RYE MIX:
1 cup (240g) boiling water (400%)
½ cup (60g) rye flour (100%)

FOR THE DOUGH:
7oz (200g) rye leaven at 70°F (67%)
3 tbsp (50g) cold water at 66°F (17%)
10½oz (300g) hot gelatinized rye mix (100%)
2½ cups (300g) fine rye flour (100%)
1 tsp fine sea salt (2%)

FOR THE GELATINIZED RYE MIX Cool the boiling water until it reaches 194°F. Quickly beat in the rye flour trying to avoid too many lumps forming. Cover the bowl and leave for 1 hour (or up to 24 hours). This produces the gelatinized rye mixture that will give the crumb of the loaf some elasticity.

FOR THE DOUGH Make a rye leaven using the recipe for making a leaven (see pages 25–27) but substituting rye flour for bread flour at each step. Or take some of your white starter and refresh that using solely rye flour and water for a few days. But remember that rye flour needs more liquid to reach the same consistency as a batter made with white flour.

Beat the rye leaven into the cold water, then beat in the gelatinized rye mix (saving 1–2 tbsp to brush over the loaf). Stir this with the dry ingredients until you have a soft sticky paste. Tip this dough out onto a lightly oiled (with corn or olive oil) work-surface and knead gently into a ball. Shape the dough into a baton (see page 21). Place the loaf seam-side-up on a floured cloth, pulling the cloth up around the dough to hold its shape (or use a dusted rising basket). Allow to rise at room temperature for 5 hours, or until the loaf has almost doubled in size.

Preheat the oven to 410°F. Carefully upturn the loaf onto a baking sheet and brush with the gelatinized rye mixture. Spray the loaf lightly with water, and bake for 50 minutes, spraying the loaf again after the first 5 minutes. Allow to cool on a wire rack. When cold, wrap in parchment paper, tied well with string, and leave for a day before slicing.

Russia

If you are to believe everything you hear and read, Moscow is entering a golden moment, comparable to Berlin in the early 1970s. Old ways sit bang up against big-time modern-living, as restaurateurs and chefs, designers and architects, try to claim a piece of the easy money. The baguette and the croissant, those early warning markers of infringing western values, are starting to appear in truck stops and cafés. But if you look carefully, there are still remarkable breads around, baked using methods and ingredients unusual to us. The likelihood is, however, that these will disappear before people learn to value and preserve them.

Nina Vladimirovna Gorkovenko teaches at Yasnaya Poliana, Tolstoy's grand house in Tula, about 200 miles to the south of Moscow. The place has been preserved as a weekend attraction for Russians, and her job is to teach and demonstrate old ways to groups of visiting children. This is a sort of baking theater, an enactment of a life that faded around the 1960s, when the sudden proliferation of state-run bakeries started to provide bread for most people.

We sit in a two-roomed wooden house to which Tolstoy would retreat to write, in a building similar to Nina's childhood home. The main room contains the oven, a large beast covered in white tiles, which served both to warm the family and to cook on. Above it is a sleeping platform, a few feet below the wooden ceiling, where the family would have slept together. Underneath the oven is a small space to dry the wood, where the chickens slept at

THIS PAGE, CLOCKWISE FROM TOP LEFT: a braise of rabbit cooked in sour cream, pickled mushrooms and cucumbers; a horse-pulled sledge over snow-covered grain fields; the front of Tolstoy's *izba;* food historian Galina Ivanovna Poskrebysheva; a traditional Uzbekistan bread.
OPPOSITE PAGE, CLOCKWISE FROM TOP LEFT: the hands of Nina Vladimirovna Gorkovenko; chickens in the snow; Andrei Stephanovich Peryakin holding the wheat loaf; wheat and rye loaves rising in a pan at Andrei's house; Claudia Alexandrovna; risen wheat dough being scraped into the pan; Farkhat and Saodat; a wheat loaf in the wood-fired oven; CENTER, LEFT TO RIGHT: sheets of *matzah* (a dry unleavened bread); the wheat loaf. OVERLEAF: The path to Tolstoy's house; coriander rye at Galina's restaurant.

> "If we ran out of bread we'd get some from our neighbors. In Russia, there are few people who wouldn't share their bread with you." N. VLADIMIROVNA

night. In a corner opposite the oven is the traditional icon, an image of the Virgin Mary in a gilded wooden frame. The front windows face into the curved path of the winter sun that moves low across the horizon.

We are baking together so that I can learn to prepare the traditional oven and watch Nina mix the dough, by hand on a wooden table. "Both my mother and my grandmother used to make dark rye bread each week, and wheat bread on special occasions," said Nina. "I'd help them bake the bread then. There was no other option, as there were no small bakeries, nor anywhere to buy bread. We would grow rye and wheat, and grind it at the collective's mill. Every two or three days my mother would bake six or seven loaves—round loaves each a foot wide by five or six inches high.

"We'd use water if we had water, or milk, or even juice from the cucumber pickle or a little cabbage brine. And if we ran out of bread, we'd get some from our neighbors. In Russia, there are very few people who wouldn't share their bread with you. But, you know, I remember that we were so very happy when we could buy bread. Baking bread was hard work but I think that, like the kneading of the dough, the effort gave people resilience."

Farkhat, a chef in Moscow, and his wife Saodat are a young Uzbek couple living in an old state housing block near the center of Moscow. They left Tashkent, known as "the city of bread," to find work, leaving their four-year-old daughter behind with their parents. Together we are baking two breads, one a hat-shaped disc of almost unleavened bread and the other a fried flat bread with a dough mixed with onions and larded with small chunks of beef fat, which melt during the cooking, making the texture slightly flaky and oily. "When a young man in Uzbekistan leaves his family and goes to war," Saodat tells me as she shapes a disc of dough into the round, hat-shaped loaf on the table, "he takes a bite from the crust and his father will hang the loaf on the wall as a charm to help him return home safely. So if he returns, he will eat the remaining bread."

I traveled out to the very edges of Moscow, on a three-hour drive through snow-fields, in an old Russian army vehicle, until I reached a little huddle of cottages. At one end is the small, wooden home of Claudia Alexandrovna, the 79-year-old *babushka* (grandmother) who still helps her family bake bread. The leaven was mixed the day before, then mixed into a wheat loaf early the next morning, to be baked in an old saucepan alongside two small rye loaves in oblong bread pans. We wrap the dough-laden tins in thick cloths and travel up to the house of Andrei Stephanovich Peryakin, the godfather to her son Pavel. Andrei had built his own house, a large beautiful wooden home with stables for chickens and rabbits, and inside is a big wood-fired oven in which we'd bake. After the loaves had cooled, we ate a feast of chickens cooked in cream, pickled wild mushrooms, and large fat cucumbers in brine, washed down with sloe vodka made with berries from the garden soaked in grain spirit.

Back in Moscow, I went to visit Galina Ivanovna Poskrebysheva, a respected Russian food writer whose books sell over a million copies per edition. She has a small restaurant where forgotten regional foods are reconstructed and promoted. I asked Galina about the rise in government bakeries in the 1960s. She explained how, since bread was a staple, the government had long tried to make people healthy through maintaining its quality. Every region in Russia had its own bread, made from the local grain, and to make the state bread, government officers collected samples and recipes from each region and used them as the model for their production.

Galina asked a waiter in her restaurant to bring us a slice of one of the regional breads made by her baker Gennady Ivanov. This bread came from a 200-year-old recipe found in the State archives. The whole grain, including the husks, has been left to sprout, then pounded into a paste and mixed with a natural leaven. The taste is sweet and grassy, more vegetable than grain.

"But the bread that is made now, over the past few years, has gotten much worse," she says, somewhat angrily. "Before, the government looked after the bakeries. But after *perestroika*, the government allowed companies to come in and take over the bakeries. Now profit rather than quality is the aim."

MAIZE | THE NATURAL LEAVEN

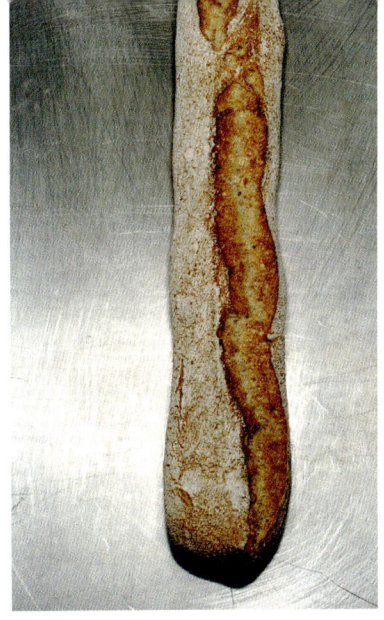

White corn and wheat loaf

8oz (230g) white leaven at 68°F (46%) (see pages 25–27)

1⅓ cups (325g) whey (or yogurt and water to make up the quantity) at 68°F (65%)

2½ cups (300g) Italian "00" flour (60%)

1 scant cup (100g) whole-wheat flour (20%)

¾ cup (100g) white corn flour (20%)

1½ tsp fine sea salt (2%)

Corn is found in many different varieties and colors, from a deep rusty purple through golden yellow and white. Though the paler corn makes less visually appetizing cornmeal, it isn't lacking in flavor and gives a good crunch to the crust of this loaf. The combination of leaven and whey helps the loaf rise quickly and tastes delicious. Either get whey by straining yogurt or curds through cheesecloth, or save the briny liquid that you find in a package of mozzarella (and cut the quantity of salt in the recipe by a third).

TIP If you can't find white corn, any other color will work just fine. Try making curds and whey by mixing a little natural or vegetarian rennet with warm milk, leaving it to stand for 1 hour, then straining it through cheesecloth overnight. Lightly salt the curds, mix with a few chopped fresh herbs, then pack into an earthenware pot. Serve as you would any soft cheese.

8.00AM In a large bowl, beat the leaven with the whey (or water and yogurt mixture). Add the Italian "00" flour, whole-wheat flour, corn flour, and salt, and stir together with your hands until you have a soft, sticky mass. The dough temperature should be about 70°F. Scrape any remaining dough from your hands, cover, and leave for 10 minutes.

8.10AM Remove the dough from the bowl and place on a lightly oiled (with corn or olive oil) or flour-dusted work-surface. Knead the dough for 10–15 seconds. Clean and dry the bowl, give it a light rub inside with oil or butter, return the dough to the bowl and leave for 10 minutes.

8.20AM Knead the dough for 10–15 seconds, shape into a ball, and then place the dough back in the bowl. Cover and leave at room temperature (around 68°F) for an additional 10 minutes.

8.30AM Knead the dough for 10–15 seconds, shape into a ball, and then place the dough back in the bowl. Cover and leave for 30 minutes.

9.00AM Knead the dough for 10–15 seconds, shape into a ball, and then place the dough back in the bowl. Cover and leave for 1 hour.

10.00AM Knead the dough for 10–15 seconds, shape into a ball, and then place the dough back in the bowl. Cover and leave for 1 hour.

11.00AM Divide the dough into two pieces, each roughly 1lb 2oz (500g) in weight. Shape each piece into a ball, cover, and leave on the work-surface for 15 minutes. Prepare two dishtowels, rubbing them with flour, then lay them on a tray.

11.15AM Shape the dough into long sticks (see page 21), and then place each seam-side-up on the flour-dusted cloth (or linen-lined baskets). Cover the upper surface with another cloth, and leave at room temperature (68°F) until almost doubled in height—about 2–2½ hours, as the whey hastens the speed the dough matures at.

1.30PM Preheat the oven to 425°F. Dust a baking sheet, or a peel if you are using an oven stone, with semolina and upturn the sticks onto this. Using a sharp blade, cut along the length of the sticks. Spray with water and bake for 50–60 minutes. Cool on a wire rack.

Barley and rye bread

Both barley and rye lack the stretchy gluten needed to hold the shape of a bold, jaunty loaf. But use them with white bread flour, and let them serve submissively as a background flavor, sour with rye and dusty with barley, and you have the perfect, friendly bread.

TIP To enhance the nutty flavor of the barley flour, toast it lightly in a 350°F oven for 15 minutes, then cool before using. Simmered and soaked grains of rye and barley, well drained, can also be added to the mix.

9oz (250g) rye leaven at 68°F (50%)
1¼ cups (300g) water at 68°F (60%)
2 cups (300g) bread flour (60%)

1 scant cup (100g) rye flour (20%)
1 scant cup (100g) barley flour (20%)
1½ tsp fine sea salt (2%)

To make the rye leaven, see pages 25–27 and 31.

8.00AM In a large bowl, beat the rye leaven with the water. Next, mix in the bread flour, rye flour, barley flour, and salt, and stir together with your hands until you have a soft, sticky mass. The dough temperature should be about 70°F. Scrape any remaining dough from your hands, cover, and leave for 10 minutes.

8.10AM Remove the dough from the bowl and place on a lightly oiled (with corn or olive oil) or flour-dusted work-surface. Knead the dough for 10–15 seconds. Clean and dry the bowl, give it a light rub inside with oil or butter, return the dough to the bowl and leave for 10 minutes.

8.20AM Knead the dough for 10–15 seconds, shape into a ball, and then place the dough back in the bowl. Cover and leave at room temperature (around 68°F) for an additional 10 minutes.

8.30AM Knead the dough for 10–15 seconds, shape into a ball, and then place the dough back in the bowl. Cover and leave for 30 minutes.

9.00AM Knead the dough for 10–15 seconds, shape into a ball, and then place the dough back in the bowl. Cover and leave for 1 hour.

10.00AM Knead the dough for 10–15 seconds, shape into a ball, and then place the dough back in the bowl. Cover and leave for 1 hour.

11.00AM Divide the dough into two pieces, each roughly 1lb 2oz (500g) in weight. Shape each piece into a ball, cover, and leave for 15 minutes. Prepare dishtowels, rubbing them with flour, then using them to line two bowls (20cm wide), or use flour-dusted, linen-lined baskets.

11.15AM Shape the dough into balls, then place each seam-side-up on the flour-dusted cloth (or linen-lined baskets). Cover the upper surface with another cloth, and leave at room temperature (68°F) until almost doubled in height—about 5 hours.

4.30PM Preheat the oven to 425°F. Dust a baking sheet, or a peel if you are using an oven stone, with semolina and upturn a loaf onto this. Cut a square shape in the top of the loaf using a sharp blade. Spray the top of the loaf with water, and bake for 50–60 minutes. Cool on a wire rack. Bake the remaining loaf using the same method, or bake them at the same time if there is enough room in the oven.

Sprouted and malted grains

Sugars, stored as starch within a grain, are the plant's way of providing food for the seedling that will grow in the spring. It takes a simple process involving enzymes to convert these starches into a form the seedling can utilize. It was probably by chance that people first noticed that sprouted grains tasted sweeter when lightly roasted in a dry oven. This process of sprouting and roasting is called malting.

Many grains can be malted: wheat, barley, rye, spelt. Most of the demand for malted grains today is from the brewing industry, as malt gives beer its rich golden color. In bread-making, malt will overcome some of the depletion in sugar that occurs in slowly fermented breads—a depletion that causes the loaf to lack color even after a long bake and, when sliced, to toast and brown very slowly.

Malting is a skilled craft, and for anyone using a large quantity of malt, it is best to take advantage of the malted grains available from brewer's merchants or a local maltster. Mail order is always possible, and it is easy to find a supplier through the internet. But should you want to understand the process involved, and to become accepting of malt's natural place in the palette of ingredients used in bread-making, try making a simple malt at home, which is suited to the less demanding needs of the home baker.

Bitter hops and barm

The maltose that forms naturally in the grain is rapidly utilized by the budding yeast cells, but also by other less friendly bacteria and fungi. If an infusion made from hops is added to the mash, then its mild antiseptic properties will keep the ferment sweetly fragrant. Hops give beer its slight bitterness, and were once used by both brewers and bakers to ward off a disagreeable sourness. Bakers would use a modified beer-making process, known as a "barm," beating flour into a hot, liquid mix of hops and malt so that the starch gelatinized. This proved a perfect medium for fermentation once seeded with a little of the barm from a previous week's baking. This mixture could be kept for a week, as the bitter hops would keep the mixture sweet tasting.

Until the 20th century, when the use of commercial yeast became commonplace, bakers struggled to make bread as cleanly flavored and white as they could. Sourness was considered a bad thing, and papers and essays were written advising bakers on how best to avoid it. The newly available processed yeast made it possible to mix and bake dough quickly which meant that the bacteria did not have time to develop and sour the loaf. Bakers rejoiced except a few.

In Scotland, for example, the bakers weren't so taken with this new, clean-tasting bread. Comparing the two breads, one made in the old style with barm, and another with the new-fangled yeast, both bakers and customers preferred the old style. But barm-making was laborious, and the new yeast convenient. And convenience won.

Sprouting and home malting

Take 1 cup (200g) of clean barley, and soak it for 6 hours in cold water at 59–66°F (in my home, I get that temperature in the area under the sink). Pour the barley into a strainer and allow it to drain for 4 hours, stirring it occasionally with a spoon so that it dries evenly. Steep the grain once more in cold water (at 59–66°F) for 8 hours, then pour again through a strainer and transfer onto cheesecloth or paper towel. Cover the grains with another piece of cheesecloth (or paper towel).

Keep at 59–66°F for 4–5 days, making sure the grains stay moist with water, but not covered. Rinse the seeds once a day in fresh cold water to keep them clean. Dry in a warm room for 12 hours, then place them in an oven at its lowest setting (somewhere between 120–160°F, check with your oven thermometer) for 2–3 hours in order to lightly brown the grains, anything from golden to chocolate. Allow to cool and store in an airtight jar.

To use, grind the required amount in a coffee grinder, and add to your flour mix.

TO HOME MALT BARLEY it needs to be soaked in cold water and then allowed to dry several times over the course of a few days.

SOAKED BARLEY DRYING on a cheesecloth or paper towel.

ONCE YOUR BARLEY IS READY TO USE grind the amount you need in a coffee grinder and add to your flour mix.

A quicker barm

The home mashing of malt is tricky, as it is difficult to hold the mashing liquid at the right temperature. If you are interested, then a home brewing supplier can provide you with all the ingredients needed. But there is another way. A live, bottle-conditioned ale, gently heated to 158°F, can have flour beaten into it. This is a perfect replication of the complex barm of old, and once seeded with a little of your leaven, will make excellent bread. Traditionally, the fermented barm would have been mixed with a small quantity of flour from the total amount, and when this had fermented it was incorporated into the rest of the ingredients. This reduced the bitterness from the hops and produced a whiter, cleaner tasting loaf. But I don't mind the slight bitterness, so the recipe in this book skips this intermediate stage.

1 cup (250g) bottle-conditioned beer or ale (500%)
⅓ cup (50g) bread flour (100%)
4 tsp white leaven (40%) (see pages 25–27)

Heat the beer or ale to 58°F in a saucepan, then remove from the heat and quickly beat in the flour, aiming to have as few lumps as possible. Transfer to a small bowl (that the mixture will half fill), and allow to cool. When the temperature has dropped to 68°F, stir in the leaven. Cover and leave overnight, by which time it should be fermenting. Use as you would a leaven (though reduce the water accordingly in the recipe as the barm is quite liquid).

Barm bread

This is the traditional wheaten bread of England. It uses the barm described opposite as the leavening agent. Simply mix this with flour, water, and salt, allow to rise, and then bake in a hot oven. The loaf is very simple to make, and richly flavored from the beer-based barm, which has a slight bitterness from the green hops, and sweetness from the malted and toasted barley.

TIP Try making the barm with different beers or ales, but always look for traditional bottle-conditioned brews. Alter the flour mix, using wholewheat, rye, and barley, and try simmering wholegrains in water before giving them a soak overnight in ale or mead, then drain them thoroughly before adding to the dough.

5½oz (150g) barm (see opposite) (30%)
1 cup (250g) water at 68°F (50%)
3⅔ cups (500g) bread flour (100%)
1½ tsp fine sea salt (2%)

8.00AM In a large bowl, beat the barm with the water. Add the bread flour and salt, and stir together with your hands until you have a soft, sticky mass. The dough temperature should be about 70°F. Scrape any remaining dough from your hands, cover, and leave for 10 minutes.

8.10AM Remove the dough from the bowl and place on a lightly oiled or flour-dusted work-surface. Knead the dough for 10–15 seconds. Clean and dry the bowl, give it a light rub inside with oil or butter, return the dough to the bowl and leave for 10 minutes.

8.20AM Knead the dough for 10–15 seconds, shape into a ball, and then place the dough back in the bowl. Cover and leave at room temperature (around 68°F) for an additional 10 minutes.

8.30AM Knead the dough for 10–15 seconds, shape into a ball, and then place the dough back in the bowl. Cover and leave for 30 minutes.

9.00AM Knead the dough for 10–15 seconds, shape into a ball, and then place the dough back in the bowl. Cover and leave for 1 hour.

10.00AM Knead the dough for 10–15 seconds, shape into a ball, and then place the dough back in the bowl. Cover and leave for 1 hour.

11.00AM Knead the dough for 10–15 seconds, shape into a ball, and then place the dough back in the bowl. Cover and leave for 2 hours.

1.00PM Divide the dough into two pieces, each roughly 1lb (450g) in weight. Shape each piece into a ball, cover, and leave on the work-surface for 15 minutes. Prepare two dishtowels, rubbing them with flour, then using them to line two bowls (8in wide), or use flour-dusted, linen-lined baskets.

1.15PM Shape the dough once more into balls, then place each seam-side-up in the flour-dusted cloths (or linen-lined baskets). Cover the upper surface with another cloth, and leave at room temperature (68°F) until almost doubled in height.

5.30PM Preheat the oven to 425°F. Dust a baking sheet, or a peel if you are using an oven stone, with semolina and upturn one loaf onto this. Using a sharp blade, cut two slashes across the loaf in the shape of a cross. Spray the top of the loaf with water, and bake for 50–70 minutes. Cool on a wire rack. Bake the remaining loaf using the same method, or bake them at the same time if there is enough room in the oven.

Crusty potato bread

9oz (250g) white leaven (50%) (see pages 25–27)
1¼ cups (300g) water at 68°F (60%)
1 tbsp honey (5%)

3oz (75g) grated scrubbed and unpeeled potato (15%)
3⅔ cups (500g) bread flour (100%)
1½ tsp fine sea salt (2%)

8.00AM In a large bowl, beat the leaven with the water, honey, and grated potato. Add the flour and salt, and stir together with your hands until you have a soft, sticky mass. The dough temperature should be about 70°F. Scrape any remaining dough from your hands, cover, and leave for 10 minutes.

8.10AM Remove the dough from the bowl and place on a lightly oiled (with olive oil) or flour-dusted work-surface. Knead for 10–15 seconds. Clean the bowl, give it a light rub with oil or butter, return the dough to the bowl and leave for 10 minutes.

8.20AM Knead for 10–15 seconds, shape into a ball, then place the dough back in the bowl. Cover and leave at room temperature (about 68°F) for 10 minutes.

8.30AM Knead the dough for 10–15 seconds, shape into a ball, and then place the dough back in the bowl. Cover and leave for 30 minutes.

9.00AM Knead the dough for 10–15 seconds, shape into a ball, and then place the dough back in the bowl. Cover and leave for 1 hour.

10.00AM Knead the dough for 10–15 seconds, shape into a ball, and then place the dough back in the bowl. Cover and leave for 1 hour.

11.00AM Knead the dough for 10–15 seconds, shape into a ball, and then place the dough back in the bowl. Cover and leave for 1 hour.

12.00 MIDDAY Divide the dough into two pieces, each roughly 1¼lb (550–600g). Shape each piece into a ball, cover, and leave for 15 minutes. Rub a dishtowel with flour, then lay it on a large tray, or use a flour-dusted, linen-lined basket.

12.15PM Sit a ball of dough seam-side-upwards on the floured work-surface (see page 20). Pat it flat with your hands, then take the left and right sides furthest from you, and fold them toward the center by ¾in, making a triangular point. Take that point and fold it inward to the center, pressing it down to seal. Rotate the dough 180°, then repeat with the other side. Rotate the dough, back to the start position. If you are right-handed, fold the dough in half toward you starting at the right-hand end, sealing the dough with the heel of your right hand while holding and folding it with your left. Roll the shaped loaf with both hands around it, pressing slightly more with the heel of each hand to give the ends a point. Place the dough seam-side-up on the cloth. Fold and pull the cloth up the sides of the loaf (if using a linen-lined basket, just place the dough seam-side-up inside). Repeat with the remaining dough and sit this next to the first, separated by the cloth. Cover with a cloth, and leave at room temperature (68°F) until almost doubled in height—about 4½–5 hours.

5.00–5.30PM Preheat the oven to 425°F. Dust a baking sheet, or peel if you're using an oven stone, with semolina. Upturn one loaf onto the tray, and make a cut along the loaf's length. Spray the top of the loaf with water, and bake for 50–70 minutes. Cool on a wire rack. Bake the remaining loaf using the same technique.

This is a strongly flavored crusty loaf that keeps moist with the grated potato and fragrant with the hint of honey. The sourness of the leaven base combines well with the two, making this a rather fine naturally leavened loaf.

From water to wine

If you have any sense of economy, you will find that wasting food is painful. At times we all have more than we want of some things—more sun or more rain—and not every surplus can be turned to benefit. But we can be considered in our approach to meager or lavish resources, using them respectfully and carefully.

If there is a little wine or beer left over after a bottle is opened and cooked grains remaining from a meal—a spoonful of lentils, some scrapings of rice—they can sit together in a bowl so that their flavors combine. Left overnight, these grains will plump up into juicy seeds that will moisten and hearten a whole-grain loaf. Make use of apples from a tree that is old and productive; they will need harvesting, and their flesh and sweet juice can be used in foods if we are to make the best from the crop.

On a farm, the importance of economy is more apparent. When milk is fresh and warm from the cow, it will separate into thick cream and light milk. If that milk sours, the heavy curds can be collected and salted to make cheese. The remaining opalescent liquid, called whey, can be used to create a simple loaf. No part need be wasted, discarded or poured down the drain.

It can happen in reverse. My mother would sometimes open wine when cooking the evening meal in order to add a dash to a sauce or a braise. A flagon of hard cider can both be used in making bread in the morning, and to drink a salute to the loaf after baking.

Water is not the only liquid we can, or should, use in bread-making. If I have water, then I will use water. But if I have other good things that need using up, then I will make the best use of them every time.

Whey bread with butter and honey

Where to get whey? If you stir a little rennet into warm milk, the resulting curds can be strained through layers of cheesecloth to make a simple soft cheese. The watery liquid drained off is called whey, and has traditionally been used as a liquid to make bread with. It can be either sweet or sour, depending on the condition of the milk it was strained from. It can be left over from cheese- or butter-making, or after straining yogurt.

TIP Fromage frais, a fresh soft cheese, can be beaten into cold milk (5½oz/150g cheese to 2 cups/500g milk) and left overnight to sour. The following day, gently warm the sour milk so that curds form. Strain the milk through a cloth for a few hours, then lightly salt the remaining curd in the cloth (½tsp fine sea salt for every 1lb 2oz/500g curd).

FOR THE SOFT CHEESE AND WHEY:
3 cups (750g) milk
1 tsp rennet

FOR THE DOUGH:
1½ tsp fresh yeast, crumbled (2%)
1¼ cups (300g) whey (60%)
2 tbsp honey (10%)
3⅔ cups (500g) bread flour (100%)
1¼ tsp fine sea salt (2%)
¼ cup (50g) softened butter (10%)

FOR THE WHEY: Warm the milk to blood temperature (98°F). Remove from the heat. Transfer to a glass bowl and stir in the rennet quickly and evenly. Leave undisturbed in a warm place for 1 hour, so the milk solidifies into a large curd. If you gently shake the bowl, the contents should shimmer rather than cause waves. This is the old-fashioned English dessert "junket." Using a butter knife, cut the curds into small pieces. Tip both curds and whey into a colander or strainer lined with cheesecloth set over a bowl. Refrigerate.

The following day, either lightly salt the strained curds, or leave them unsalted and sweet. Stir the curds together, and pack into a bowl lined with more cheesecloth. You can spread nuggets of this soft cheese on a crisp cracker or on a soft slice cut from a freshly baked loaf. With the remaining whey, make a loaf of bread.

FOR THE DOUGH: In a bowl beat the yeast with the whey and honey. Stir in half the flour and the salt, and leave in a warm place for 30 minutes, to make a yeast batter.

Meanwhile, rub the butter into the remaining flour, until it is evenly incorporated and the mixture resembles fine bread crumbs. Stir in the yeast batter after its 30 minute rest, and mix together until you have a soft dough. Scrape any remaining dough from your hands, cover the bowl and leave for 10 minutes. Rub 1 tsp of corn or olive oil on the work-surface and knead the dough for 10 seconds, ending with the dough in a smooth, round ball. Wipe the bowl clean and rub with 1 tsp olive oil, return the dough to it, cover and leave for 10 minutes. Repeat this light kneading twice more, at 10 minute intervals, then leave the dough for 30 minutes.

At this stage the dough should be soft and elastic, with air bubbles starting to show as blisters on the outer surface. A quick small cut through the surface of the dough should show a network of air bubbles created by the yeast. Shape the dough into a ball (see page 21), and place it smooth-side down into a flour-dusted cloth. Leave in a warm place (68–75°F) for 1 hour.

Preheat the oven to 425°F. Upturn the dough onto a flour-dusted baking sheet, then gently spray the outside of the dough with water. Place the tray in the center of the oven and bake for 50 minutes, or until the loaf is a good brown color and light in weight. Cool on a wire rack.

Simple milk loaf

Soft and good for a sandwich, this milk bread contains sugars that also make it perfect for toasting. Much like the pain de mie from France, the English milk loaf has a homely appearance. But unlike the controlled look and delicate structure of the Gallic loaf, this bread relies on the thrust created by glutinous bread flour to jump boldly over the top of the tin. Its strong, slightly tough crumb will make a jelly sandwich that can withstand the rigors of a child's schoolbag, or a cheese sandwich that can survive in a jogger's backpack.

1½ tsp fresh yeast, crumbled (2%)
1½ cups (350g) whole milk at 68°F (70%)
1 tbsp corn or maple syrup (4%)
2 cups (250g) all-purpose flour (50%)
1¾ cups (250g) bread flour (50%)
1¼ tsp fine sea salt (2%)
2 tbsp warm melted unsalted butter

In a large bowl, beat the yeast with the milk and syrup. Add the flours and the salt, and squidge the lot together with your hands until you have a soft, sticky dough and the flour and liquid have evenly combined. Pour over the warm melted butter, and then squeeze this into the dough. Scrape any remaining dough from your hands, cover the bowl and leave for 10 minutes. Rub 1 tsp of olive or corn oil on the work-surface and knead the dough for 10 seconds, ending with the dough in a smooth round ball. Wipe the bowl clean and rub with 1 tsp olive oil, return the dough to it, cover and leave for an additional 10 minutes. Repeat this light kneading twice more, at 10 minute intervals, then leave the dough for 30 minutes.

Grease and flour a deep loaf pan (4½x 7½in). Divide the dough into two equal pieces and shape each into a ball. Drop them side-by-side into the prepared pan, cover with a cloth, and allow to rise for 1½ hours, or until almost doubled in height.

Preheat the oven to 410°F. Brush the top of the loaf with a little cream or milk, and bake for 15 minutes, then lower the heat to 350°F and bake for an additional 25–30 minutes, or until the top of the loaf is a shiny dark brown, and the loaf has come away from the sides of the pan. Remove from the pan, and allow to cool on a wire rack.

Ale bread with wheat grains

Beer-making and bread-making have existed side-by-side for centuries. In Italy, bakers' yeast is still referred to as lievito di birra, and the barm-making practice that lasted in Scotland well into the 20th century used a modified beer recipe, in which flour was whisked into the hot liquid left from the mashing of malted grains and the boiling of hops. These hops gave the liquid slight anti-bacterial properties, and helped keep the ferment from souring (for much of our baking history, the aim was to ferment dough rather than to sour it). Now we rely on lactic ferments to protect our food from more harmful bacteria, a form of natural preservation. But enough. The beer-soaked grains used here are simply good to eat, and their moistness helps keep the crumb sticky-soft for many days.

2 cups (300g) bread flour (60%)
1¼ cup (150g) rye flour (30%)
½ cup (50g) whole-wheat bread flour (10%)
1½ tsp fine sea salt (2%)
¾ cup (200g) ale (40%)
6 tbsp (100g) water at 68°F (20%)
10½oz (300g) white leaven (60%) (see pages 25–27)
¾ tsp fresh yeast, crumbled (1%)
⅓oz (10g) ground malted grains (2%) (see page 39)
7oz (200g) cooked wheat grains (40%), (see opposite, but soaked overnight in ale rather than wine)

Combine the three flours, and mix with the salt. In another bowl, beat the ale and water with the leaven and yeast, together with the ground malt and ale-soaked wheat. Then add the flour. Mix both together with your hands, squeezing it through your fingertips. When roughly combined, cover the bowl and leave it for 10 minutes. Knead gently on a lightly oiled surface for 10–15 seconds, until combined. Return the dough to the bowl, leave for an additional 30 minutes, then knead once more for a further 10–15 seconds.

Give the dough a turn (see page 19), and repeat the turning after 30 minutes and 1 hour. Dust a dishtowel with rye flour, and line an 8-cup bowl with this (or use a flour-dusted rising basket). Shape the dough into a ball and place seam-side-up in the cloth. Cover and leave for 2 hours, or until doubled in size.

Preheat the oven to 410°F. Carefully upturn the dough onto a flour-dusted baking sheet, and cut a series of slashes across the upper surface. Bake in the center of the oven for 45 minutes, until the loaf is a good rich brown in color and, when tapped on the bottom, sounds hollow. Allow to cool on a wire rack.

Alsace loaf with rye

The crisp fruitiness of an Alsace wine provides a gentle marinade for the cooked rye grains. Sometimes these grains are called "berries," and the description makes sense when you taste them cooked in this way. The rye grains swell and soften during the initial cooking in water, and then overnight the wine plumps up each grain and adds a slightly sharp sweetness, and you can happily eat the grains by the handful. If you don't want to use alcohol, then replace this marinade with either thin yogurt or a good cold-pressed fruit juice.

FOR THE GRAINS (makes 10½oz (300g) of soaked grains):

7oz (200g) whole rye grains

water to cover

¾ cup (200g) white wine

FOR THE DOUGH:

2½ cups (350g) bread flour (70%)

1 scant cup (100g) whole-wheat flour (20%)

½ cup (50g) rye flour (10%)

1⅓ cups (325g) water at 68°F (65%)

¾ tsp fresh yeast, crumbled (1%)

1½ tbsp honey (5%)

5½oz (150g) rye leaven (30%)

(see pages 25–27 and 31)

10½oz (300g) wine-soaked grains, drained (60%)

1¼ tsp fine sea salt (3%)

2 tbsp melted butter, lard, or oil (5%)

FOR THE GRAINS In a small saucepan, mix the rye grains with the water. Bring the mixture to a boil, then lower the heat and simmer for 45 minutes, if necessary topping the saucepan up with extra water so that the grains are always covered by liquid. Remove from the heat, transfer the grains and remaining cooking liquid to a container and, when cool, strain (this liquid can be used in place of the water in the recipe) and cover with wine (or yogurt or juice). Place in the refrigerator, or another cool place, overnight. Drain before use.

FOR THE DOUGH Mix the flours lightly together and leave to one side. In a second bowl, place the water, fresh yeast, and honey, stir well and leave the mixture to sit for 10 minutes. Add the leaven (broken into small pieces) and grains to the yeasted mixture. Stir this mixture into the dry ingredients, then mix together well with your hands, squeezing it through your fingertips. When roughly combined, cover the bowl and leave it for 10 minutes. Tip the dough out onto a lightly floured work-surface, sprinkle over the salt and melted butter, and knead gently for 10–15 seconds, until combined. Return the dough to the bowl, leave for an additional 30 minutes, then knead once more for an additional 10–15 seconds.

Give the dough a turn (see page 19), and repeat every half hour for 1½ hours (do not turn it at the end of this time). Divide the dough into five pieces, each just over 9oz (250g). Roll each piece into a stick or baton (see page 21), lay each seam-side-up on a flour-dusted cloth, and allow to rise for 1 hour.

Preheat the oven to 410°F. Carefully upturn two or three of the sticks of dough out onto a flour-dusted baking sheet, and cut three or four slashes diagonally across the upper surface. Bake in the center of the oven for 35 minutes, until the sticks are a good rich brown color, and when tapped on the bottom, sound hollow. Allow to cool on a wire rack and bake the remaining bread.

Ukraine

Yaroslava Kharuk, her son Andrei, and their Rottweiler, Jack, live in a 1950s block in the Ukraine city of Ivano-Frankivsk in a three-room apartment with a small kitchen annex. Jack is a bear of a dog, his coat shines and his eyes are bright. He's fed bread and gravy, or cabbage and potatoes, cooked at the same time as the evening meal. Yaroslava cooks with little waste. Scraps are fed to Jack or used in other dishes. Most of the ingredients come from her parents' farm, with soft cheese and milk from the family cow and carrots and potatoes from the fields her father has plowed.

This morning's breakfast consists of fried farm eggs, each with a deep-yellow yolk, dark rye bread, fresh butter, coffee, different pork cuts, sausages, and apricot juice. Then we head for the street market to buy flour, fresh yeast, and salt.

Vans are parked with their rear doors open to display trayfuls of bread, collected by each seller from the local bakeries and supplemented with loaves baked at home and by friends. There are a dozen different rye breads, each labeled with the ingredients and price. Subtle variations between ingredients in bread are noticed and appreciated by customers in Eastern Europe, whereas in the West we have moved stridently toward bolder, more obvious contrasts in taste. Appreciating slight differences requires knowledge and some understanding of the way

LEFT PAGE, CLOCKWISE FROM TOP LEFT: Sister Joanna holds open a recipe book from the convent; the chapel ceiling at the Ukrainian Greek-Catholic Church; animals and fishermen by the river Dnister; Maria in front of her wood-fired oven; loaves sold from a van at a street market in Ivano-Frankivsk THIS PAGE, CLOCKWISE FROM TOP LEFT: Mykola Kobylansky, mayor of Pidverbchi; Sister Joanna sifting flour; plaiting dough for *paska*; *talena*, a local red berry, preserved and used as a remedy; an ornate barn; dough rising; eggs being beaten; dark rye bread with a glass of vodka steeped with *talena* berries.

FROM WATER TO WINE | UKRAINE

RIGHT: Maria uses a brush of chicken feathers;
RIGHT: Wasyl with the happy pigs in the yard.

> "If a girl married, her plait of hair would be cut and nailed to the roof of their house. Now we have a loaf." SISTER JOANNA

local history has affected each bread. The different, often symbolic, shapes of bread result in different flavors and textures, since the distance warmth must travel through the unbaked dough will affect fermentation, and the time the loaf spends in the oven will affect the flavor.

We travel near the foothills of the Carpathian Mountains to a village called Pidverbchi, where Yaroslava's parents, Maria and Wasyl, have a small farm surrounded by bare, plowed fields where the stumps of cabbage stalks stick out like stakes from the ground. "When I was 20 and married a year," Maria tells me as she puts a flame to the wood in the oven, "I had been left to bake bread. I didn't know how much wood to use, so I packed the oven full and set it alight. There were flames everywhere, and Wasyl was terrified the house would burn down. I got a bucket of water and threw it in, and that put the fire out. Then I tried to relight it, but everything was soaking. That's how I learned that bread doesn't need much wood."

Outside the house there are two wells: one that collects rainwater and the other filled by a spring in the ground. "Rainwater is softer and better for washing," says Maria, "and well-water is better for cooking." She mixes a little whey, strained from soft cheese, with yeast and a spoonful of flour. This is left for a few hours beside the oven while I walk with Wasyl and my translator, Oxana, to the river Dnister to pick berries and see what the fishermen have caught. Along the riverbank, cows and goats are grazing. Each family takes it in turn to walk the cattle to new pasture.

Back at the farmhouse, the yeast mixture is bubbling. Maria mixes it with flour, salt, eggs, and well-water to form a sticky dough. This is kneaded gently, then left to rise. An old oblong pan is greased lightly, then the dough is divided, shaped into a baton, tucked into the pan, and left to double in height. Finally, Maria goes to the yard and collects long chicken feathers. She ties these together with thread, uses them to brush a beaten egg onto the dough's surface and puts the pan in the oven. We eat the bread early that evening, with small fried potato cakes, pickled tomatoes, and local ham. The bread has a slightly sour tang and a creamy taste in the crumb. It is good and comforting.

Days later we visit the convent of the Sisters Meronocyts, part of the Ukrainian Greek-Catholic Church that reformed after *perestroika* in 1991, having been banned during the Soviet era. Part of the sisters' daily work is bread-baking, and this continued even during the years without a convent. Mother Theresa joined the convent when she was 15, before it was legal. "In 1952 the soldiers gave the sisters 24 hours to leave the convent and dismantle the church. From then on we practiced the faith in secret, meeting at one of the sister's homes and praying in the quiet of a bedroom. Every so often someone would be arrested and imprisoned."

This convent, built after *perestroika*, has a glazed-tile wood-oven. "We make enriched breads plaited and twisted into ceremonial shapes, typically for weddings, Easter, and Christmas. *Kolach* is an important bread," says Mother Teresa. "When someone dies it is usual to have a service at home. On the table there will be holy water, a loaf of *Kolach*, and a candle." The plait, too, is symbolic. Sister Joanna tells me: "My grandmother said that three years ago, when a girl married, her plait of hair would be cut and nailed to the roof of their house. Now we have a loaf, and everyone is happier."

LEFT TO RIGHT: Svetlana, Jergenia, and Avanna stock the shelves with bread at a bakery in Bogorogchany; baker Vitaliy holding a stack of light rye bread.

Scrumpy buns

In *The Book of Apples* Joan Morgan describes how during the Middle Ages "cider and ale battled for first place in the English tankard." Such was the popularity of hard cider, yet it now lags behind. The fermented juice of apples could either be brewed to a standard comparable to fine wine, or left coarse and lowly as simple "scrumpy." These large buns use the latter combined with barley and malt, giving the crumb a caramel tint and smoky flavor.

TIP You can stir 1 tsp of the leaven with sweet unpasteurized apple juice, leave it overnight, and use the subsequent fermented liquid in place of water in your bread-making.

2 cups (300g) bread flour (60%)
1⅔ cups (200g) barley flour (40%)
¼oz (10g) home malted barley, ground (2%) (see page 39)
1½ tsp fine sea salt (2%)
1⅓ cups (325g) scrumpy or hard cider (65%)
7oz (200g) white leaven (40%) (see pages 25–27)
1¼ tsp fresh yeast, crumbled (1%)
extra hard cider for brushing the loaves
flakes of sea salt to sprinkle on top

Combine the flours with the ground malted barley, and mix with the salt. In another bowl, beat the scrumpy or cider with the leaven and yeast. Mix this liquid together with the dry ingredients using your hands, squeezing it through your fingertips. When roughly combined, cover the bowl and leave for 10 minutes. Tip the dough out onto a lightly floured work-surface, and knead gently for 10–15 seconds, until combined. Return the dough to the bowl, leave for an additional 30 minutes, then knead once more for 10–15 seconds.

Give the dough a turn (see page 19), and repeat after 30 minutes and 1 hour. Divide the dough into five pieces, each weighing roughly 7oz (200g). Round each piece into a ball and sit them on a baking sheet, evenly spaced (i.e. one toward each corner and one in the middle). Cover with a cloth and allow to rise for 2 hours, or until nearly doubled in height.

Preheat the oven to 410°F. Brush the top of each bun with scrumpy (or cider) and sprinkle with salt flakes. Bake in the center of the oven for 35 minutes, until the buns are a good rich brown color and, when tapped on the bottom, sound hollow. Leave to cool on a wire rack.

Red wine loaf with pine nuts and figs

This loaf is a hybrid, and was inspired by two bakers—one I still know, and one I only have a memory of. I worked at Baker & Spice with a young Frenchman, who told me about a long walnut baton that he made by storing the nuts in good red wine, and using both the ruddied nuts and the dark wine in the loaf. The other baker, Federico Turi, made a round, crusty fig and raisin bread at Locanda Locatelli, but the mixing caused the fruit pieces to disappear, with only the flecks of tiny seeds remaining. Here, the two loaves become one in a flat disc that gives maximum crust, the crumb studded with ruby-coated pine nuts and with a crunch on the teeth from fig seeds.

FOR THE NUTS AND FIGS (makes 12oz/350g when soaked and strained):
- 1 cup (250g) red wine
- 1 cup (100g) pine nuts
- 7oz (200g) dried figs, cut into eighths

FOR THE DOUGH:
- 1¾ cups (250g) bread flour (50%)
- 2 cups (250g) whole-wheat bread flour (50%)
- 1½ tsp fine sea salt (2%)
- 1 cup plus 1 tbsp (260g) reserved wine from soaking, made up with water (52%)
- 1¼ tsp fresh yeast, crumbled (1%)
- 5½oz (150g) white leaven (30%) (see pages 25–27)
- 12oz (350g) nuts and figs, strained (70%)

FOR THE NUTS AND FIGS In a saucepan, place the wine, pine nuts, and chopped figs. Bring to a boil, then simmer for a minute. Remove from the heat and leave covered overnight, stirring the mixture once before you go to bed. Next day, strain the liquid off, reserving it and making it up to the required amount with water.

FOR THE DOUGH Combine the flours, and mix with the salt. In another bowl, beat the water (and wine) with the leaven and yeast, together with the pine nuts and figs. Mix the flour and liquid together with your hands, squeezing it through your fingertips. When roughly combined, cover the bowl and leave it for 10 minutes. Tip the dough out onto a lightly floured work-surface, and knead gently for 10–15 seconds, until combined. Return the dough to the bowl, leave for an additional 30 minutes then knead once more for 10–15 seconds.

Give the dough a turn (see page 19), and repeat after 30 minutes and 1 hour. Dust a dishtowel with rye flour and lay this over a tray. Divide the dough into two equal pieces and, using a little flour to dust the work-surface, knead each into a ball. Leave to sit, covered, on the work-surface for 5 minutes, so that the dough has a chance to soften after kneading. Next, using flour to stop the dough from sticking, roll each piece of dough out into a flat oval shape ⅜in thick. Place these side-by-side on the floured cloth, and cover with another cloth. Allow to rise for 1½ hours.

Preheat the oven to 410°F. Brush oil over the upper surface of the dough, then cut criss-cross slashes across the upper surface with a sharp knife or blade. Carefully transfer the dough to a flour-dusted baking sheet, and bake in the center of the oven for 45 minutes, until the loaf is a good rich brown color and, when tapped on the bottom, sounds hollow. Allow to cool on a wire rack.

Cucumber pickle juice rye loaf

This is a simple sour rye in which all of the souring comes from the cucumber pickle juice. It's a very good hearty bread, made darker by the toasted rye flour that colors the crumb without the need for malt or molasses. Cucumber pickle juice is simply the slightly salty, slightly vinegary juice in a jar of pickled cucumbers. Either eat the pickles before using the left-over juice or drain off the juice and replace it with water, with a little salt and vinegar added.

TIP To get the polished oak crust in the picture, make a starch paste by using 2½ tbsp rye flour mixed with ⅔ cup (150g) cold water, and beat as you heat this to boiling point. Then allow the paste to cool, thinning it with water until it is the consistency of thin pouring cream. 15 minutes before the end of baking, remove the loaf from the oven and quickly brush this over the uncut surface. Put the loaf back in the oven and finish the baking.

1⅔ cups (200g) toasted rye flour (40%) (see below)
2 cups (300g) bread flour (60%)
¾ tsp fine sea salt (1%)
1½ cups (350g) cucumber pickle juice at 68°F (70%)
1¼ tsp fresh yeast, crumbled (1%)
2 good sprigs (10g) fresh dill, chopped (2%)

To toast the rye flour, preheat the oven to 400°F. Spread the rye flour in a thin layer over a baking sheet, and bake for 15 minutes, or until the flour has turned a light tannish brown. Remove from the oven and allow to cool.

Combine the flours, and mix with the salt. In another bowl, beat the pickle juice with yeast and dill. Mix this liquid and the flour together with your hands, squeezing it through your fingertips. When roughly combined, cover the bowl and leave it for 10 minutes. Tip the dough out onto a lightly oiled (with corn or olive oil) work-surface and knead gently for 10–15 seconds. Return the dough to the bowl, leave for an additional 10 minutes, then knead once more for 10–15 seconds. Return the dough to the bowl, leave for 10 minutes again, then knead one final time for 10–15 seconds.

Give the dough a turn (see page 19), and repeat after 30 minutes and 1 hour. Divide the dough into two equal pieces, and shape each into a round. Place both on a flour-dusted baking sheet, leaving a space between for the loaves to grow. Cover and leave for 1 hour, or until doubled in size.

Preheat the oven to 410°F. Cut a slash across the center of each loaf. Bake in the center of the oven for 55 minutes, until the loaves are a good rich brown color and, when tapped on the bottom, sound hollow.

Sweet brandy buns

The British were a nation of bun eaters, but then innuendo got the better of us. Now we are happier nibbling the nipple off a *brioche à tête*. There were once great bun shops, selling the famous buns of Chelsea, Albion (with buttermilk and eggs), Exeter (with butter and eggs), Dublin (twisted with caraway and currants), and Bath (with peel and golden raisins). This is my stand to resurrect the grand tradition of the bun. Eat them with the best jelly and the softest cream.

TIP Just before baking, the buns are brushed with more brandy and dredged with superfine sugar but you could use any liquor that you have to douse the top. The Catalan *coca di forno* is brushed with anise liquor before being sprinkled with sugar and pine nuts prior to baking.

FOR THE FERMENT:
½ cup (125g) whole milk (83%)
1½ tsp fresh yeast, crumbled (2%)
¼ cup (50g) superfine sugar (33%)
1 cup (150g) bread flour (100%)
3 tbsp (50g) heavy cream (33%)

FOR THE DOUGH:
2½ cups (350g) bread flour (100%)
1½ tsp fine sea salt (3%)
½ cup (100g) butter, softened (28%)
1 medium egg (14%)
3 tbsp (50g) brandy (14%)
the ferment (110%)
extra brandy for brushing the buns
extra superfine sugar for dredging the buns

FOR THE FERMENT Beat all of the ingredients together in a large bowl, cover, and leave in a warm place (68–71°F) for 30 minutes.

FOR THE DOUGH In a bowl, mix the flour and salt together, then rub the softened butter into it until there are no lumps and the flour starts to resemble fine bread crumbs. Beat the egg and brandy into the ferment, then work the mixture into the buttered flour, squeezing it through your fingertips. When roughly combined, cover the bowl and leave it for 10 minutes. Tip the dough out onto a lightly oiled work-surface and knead gently for 10–15 seconds. Return the dough to the bowl, leave for an additional 10 minutes, then knead once more for an additional 10–15 seconds. Return the dough to the bowl, leave for an additional 10 minutes then knead one final time for 10–15 seconds.

Give the dough a turn (see page 19), and repeat after 30 minutes and 1 hour. Line two baking sheets with non-stick parchment paper (or use well-buttered brown paper). Divide the dough into 12 pieces, each weighing roughly 3oz (80g). Round each into a bun and sit them seam-side-down on the baking sheets, evenly spaced. Cover with a dry cloth and leave to rise in a cool place (59–64°F) for 1½–2 hours.

Preheat the oven to 400°F. Brush the surface of the buns with the extra brandy, then dredge them lightly with the additional superfine sugar. Bake in the center of the oven for 15 minutes, then reduce the heat to 350°F and bake for an additional 10–15 minutes, until the buns are golden brown. Allow to cool on a wire rack. When cold, place in a paper bag (or freeze) to help them stay soft.

Cassis and currant loaf

Currants are tiny dried black grapes, whereas black currants are little dark fruits from a relative of the gooseberry. But when combined in this way, their flavors unite and form a single, intense "currant" taste. For this bread, the currants are simmered gently in water and cassis, then the mixture is left overnight. The following day, the strained liquid adds sweetness and color to the loaf, while the plump currants stud the crumb. Rye and black currants are good partners, and the loaf can be made well with dried black currants. The currants and rye can also be partnered with dark red grape juice.

TIP If you have a large crop of black currants, they can be home-dried by spreading them out on a sheet of wire gauze (stretched over a square wooden frame), and left in the sun to bake until shrivelled—but not as hard as stones. Alternatively, pack them in a jar, layered with superfine sugar and then covered with vodka or *eau de vie*.

FOR THE SOAKED CURRANTS (makes 10oz (280g) when soaked and strained):
1⅔ cups (250g) currants
⅔ cup (150g) water
3 tbsp (50g) cassis

FOR THE DOUGH:
1¾ cups (250g) bread flour (50%)
1 scant cup (100g) wholewheat bread flour (20%)
1¼ cups (150g) rye flour (30%)
1½ tsp fine sea salt (2%)
10oz (280g) soaked currants, drained (56%)
⅔ cup (150g) soaking liquid plus water to make the required weight at 68°F (30%)
2 tbsp (30g) cassis at 68°F (6%)
6 tbsp (100g) water at 68°F (20%)
¾ tsp fresh yeast, crumbled (1½%)
7oz (200g) rye leaven (40%) (see pages 25–27 and 31)

FOR THE SOAKED CURRANTS Rinse the currants, then place in a saucepan and cover with the water and cassis. Bring to a boil, then remove from the heat and allow to cool overnight.

FOR THE DOUGH Combine the flours, and mix with the salt. In another bowl, beat the soaked currants with the measured soaking liquid and water, extra cassis, water, yeast, and rye leaven.

Mix this liquid with the flour and salt, squeezing it through your fingertips. When evenly combined, cover the bowl and leave it for 10 minutes. Tip the dough out onto a lightly oiled (with corn or olive oil) work-surface and knead gently for 10–15 seconds. Return the dough to the bowl, leave for an additional 10 minutes, then knead once more for an additional 10–15 seconds. Return the dough to the bowl, leave for an additional 10 minutes, then knead one final time for 10–15 seconds.

Give the dough a turn (see page 19), and repeat after 30, 60, and 90 minutes. Dust two dishtowels with rye flour, and line two oblong loaf pans (8 x 4in) with these. They will act as the rising baskets (or use flour-dusted cane rising baskets if you have them). Shape the dough into a baton (see page 21) and place each loaf seam-side-up in the cloth. Cover and leave for 2 hours, or until doubled in size. At this point, I have left the loaf overnight in the refrigerator, and it bakes perfectly the next morning.

Preheat the oven to 410°F. Carefully upturn one loaf onto a flour-dusted baking sheet, and cut a single slash down the center of the upper surface. Brush or spray water along the cut, and bake in the center of the oven for 45 minutes, until the loaf is a good rich brown color and, when tapped on the bottom, sounds hollow. Allow to cool on a wire rack. Then bake the other loaf, or put them both in the oven at the same time if there is room.

From field to mill

FROM FIELD TO MILL | INTRODUCTION

It starts with a grain. A single grain, perhaps an heirloom, is planted, harvested, and the seeds collected to be planted again, either in the late fall or the following spring, depending on the variety. It will be harvested the following summer. Once again, those seeds are collected, planted, and harvested. That single stem of wheat has now been replaced by a patch of wheat, and that single grain has become a small bag of grain. And so, once more, the new crop of seeds is planted, fed by the rain, the nutrients in the soil, and the sunlight. To be harvested and scattered into the soil once more.

Of course you could easily go to a seed merchant and buy a sack of prepared, nutrient-washed, and genetically-sturdy grain. These are the popular plants, the ones that are fashionable and trouble-free, and the ones that make money for their seller. The other grains, though, need to find a less grasping champion.

The plants that cover the land are as important to the heritage of a country as its books, music, and customs. Many have disappeared, some only remain as photographs or drawings, but a few lucky specimens lie tucked away and secure in national archives for plants and seeds. If an enterprising farmer wants to replant a local variety that has long disappeared, it is to these archives he or she must go. Sometimes seeds have traveled far, and hidden in another country's archive might be an immigrant that, through good fortune, might be replanted once more back home.

WHITE FLOUR | FROM FIELD TO MILL

Quick white loaf

This is a close-textured, soft white bread, with no pretense to be anything other than that. Make a sandwich with a peppery, in-season tomato, sea salt, and a little sweet butter. When I was a child at the beach, my aunt would make sandwiches with such a loaf, filled with garden-fresh lettuce leaves, butter, and the inevitable crunch of stray sand.

TIP The small amount of milk in this recipe helps the bread to color, and the decent amount of yeast will ensure that as the loaf rises quickly it won't lose any of the natural sugars in the wheat flour, which means that a slice of bread will toast nicely. There is a fleck of millet throughout the dough, giving the crumb a slightly creamy color.

Clean the bowl as the dough sits on the work-surface after the first knead. This applies equally to all of the breads, as it helps keep the dough free of stray hard lumps that might flake off a dirty bowl.

¾ cup (200g) whole milk at 68°F (40%)
⅔ cup (150g) water at 68°F (30%)
2 tsp fresh yeast, crumbled (2%)
1½ cups (200g) all-purpose flour (40%)
2 cups (300g) bread flour (60%)
optional: 2oz (50g) millet flakes (10%)
1½ tsp fine sea salt (2%)

Mix the milk and water together. Crumble the yeast into the liquid and beat it gently until dissolved. Combine the dry ingredients, then mix with the liquid until you have a sticky but cohesive mass. Cover the bowl with a cloth and leave for 10 minutes.

Rub 1 tsp of corn or olive oil on the work-surface and knead the dough for 10 seconds, ending with the dough in a smooth, round ball.

Clean and dry the bowl, then rub lightly with a tsp of oil. Return the dough to the bowl, cover, and leave for an additional 10 minutes.

Remove the dough and knead once more on the oiled surface, returning the shape to a smooth, round ball. Place it back in the bowl, cover, and leave for 1¼ hours in a warmish (70–77°F) place.

Divide the dough into two pieces, each weighing just over 14oz (400g). Shape each into a ball on a lightly floured surface and leave covered for 5 minutes.

Lay a flat dinner tray with a dishtowel (or use oblong baskets if you have them), and dredge heavily with flour, rubbing it into the cloth so that it is evenly spread.

Sit one ball of dough seam-side-upward on the floured work-surface. To shape the dough (see page 20), pat it flat with your hands into an oval 6in front-to-back and slightly longer left-to-right. Take the left and right sides furthest from you and fold them inward toward the center by ⅜in, making a triangular point. Next, take that same point and fold it inward to the center, pressing it firmly down to seal. Rotate the dough 180°, and repeat with the other side. Rotate the dough once more, so that you are back in the starting position.

If you are right-handed, fold the dough in half toward you starting at the right-hand end, sealing the dough with the heel of your right hand while holding and folding the dough with your left. Roll the shaped loaf (with both hands tucked around it) on the work-surface, pressing down slightly more with the heel of each hand to give the ends a gentle point. Lift the dough and place it seam-side-upward on the cloth. Finally, fold and pull the cloth up the sides of the loaf (or if using a flour-dusted basket, simply place the seam-side upward inside). Allow to rise for 1½ hours, or until almost doubled in height.

Preheat the oven to 425°F. Turn the dough onto a flour-dusted baking sheet. Using a sharp knife, cut two or three slashes in the upper surface of each. Bake for at least 45 minutes, or until each loaf is a good golden brown.

Wheatgerm bread

Early in the 20th century doctors became increasingly aware that the health of the population was built on diet. Fiber, from the grain's outer husk, has essential benefits to our digestion; it is how our body extracts the nutrients it needs to survive and grow. Should this process struggle, then our health is compromised. In this recipe, the combination of wheatgerm, wholewheat flour, and wholewheat grains, gives you as much flavor and fiber as you could wish for in a loaf, plus a rich, natural caramel color.

TIP In an act of bread-making heresy, this bread doesn't really have an initial fermentation. After kneading, the dough is left for 10 minutes before being shaped and placed in the pan, so most of the fermentation occurs once the dough is in its final shape.

Bread-making flour has a lot of strong gluten, but it is contained within the endosperm. In white flour, all that remains is the milled endosperm; in wholewheat flour this is a smaller percentage of the dry matter. Wholewheat flours should therefore be treated as if they contain less gluten, which means you need to handle the dough less and give it a shorter initial rise. This bread has an extra 25 percent wheatgerm, which lowers the gluten content further. Be gentle with the kneading, as the bran will tear the gluten if the dough is subjected to a rigorous and extended mixing.

- 1 1/2oz (40g) whole-wheat grains, plus water to cover (10%)
- ¾ cup (100g) wheatgerm (25%)
- 3½ cups (400g) whole-wheat bread flour (100%)
- ¾ tsp fine sea salt (1%)
- 1½ cups (340g) water at 68°F (85%)
- ¼ cup (60g) orange juice at 68°F (15%)
- 2 tbsp honey (10%)
- 1¾ tsp fresh yeast, crumbled (2.5%)

Place the whole-wheat grains in a small saucepan, cover with water and simmer for 30 minutes, ensuring they remain covered with water at all times. Remove from the heat, add cold water to the pan so that the grains become lukewarm, then drain. Preheat the oven to 350°F.

Pour the wheatgerm onto a clean baking sheet, and bake for 12 minutes, shaking or stirring the sheet halfway through to ensure that the germ toasts rather than burns or stays pale. Allow to cool or, if your flour is particularly cold (if the kitchen is freezing one morning, for example), tip the hot wheatgerm into the flour and toss it through with your fingers.

Put the flour, salt, and toasted wheatgerm in a large mixing bowl. In another bowl or jug, mix the measured water, orange juice, and honey, and stir in the crumbled yeast and the cooked wholewheat grains. When the yeast has dissolved, add the liquid to the dry ingredients and mix with your hands. When evenly combined, cover the bowl with a cloth and leave for 5 minutes.

Meanwhile, grease and flour a deep, narrow 3½ x 9½in loaf pan. Rub 1 tsp of corn or olive oil onto the work-surface. Remove the dough from the bowl and knead for 10 seconds. Shape the dough back into a ball, then return it to the bowl and leave for 5 minutes. Repeat the short kneading, shape into a ball once more, return to the bowl and leave for another 5 minutes. Knead the dough one final time, shape into a ball once more, and leave for 10 minutes.

Pat the dough into a flat rectangle measuring roughly 10in left-to-right x 8in front-to-back. Roll the dough inward, starting at the end furthest from you, rolling it tightly as you do. Roll the dough gently on the work-surface, then tap the ends inward so that it will drop neatly into the prepared pan.

Cover the pan with a cloth and allow to rise in a warm (70–77°F) place for 1½ hours, or until it has risen about ½in over the top of the pan. Using a sharp blade, make several diagonal slashes across the surface of the loaf.

Preheat the oven to 425°F. Place the pan in the center of the oven and bake for a minimum of 45 minutes, or until the top of the loaf is a golden brown color, and the sides of the loaf have pulled away from the pan. Remove from the oven, leave for 5 minutes, then remove from the pan and allow to cool on a wire rack. When cold, wrap in waxed paper and either freeze or eat over the following few days.

Sweet rye bread

FOR THE OVERNIGHT BATTER:
(makes 10oz/290g)
1 cup (240g) boiling water
½ cup (50g) fine rye flour

OPTIONAL SPICES:
seeds from 3 cardamom pods, crushed
1 tsp aniseed
zest of 1 orange

FOR THE DOUGH:
7oz (200g) rye leaven (67%)
    (see pages 25–27 and 31)
⅓ cup (140g) honey (47%)
3 tbsp (50g) water at 68°F (17%)
10oz (290g) overnight batter (97%)
    (see above)
2½ cups (300g) fine rye flour (100%)
1 tsp fine sea salt (2%)

FOR THE OVERNIGHT BATTER Cool the water until it reads 176°F on a thermometer. Slowly beat in the rye flour, ensuring that the mixture is free of lumps. Cover and leave overnight.

FOR THE DOUGH Beat the rye leaven, honey, and water together with the overnight batter. Add the remaining rye flour and salt. Stir until you have a thick, evenly mixed paste. As there is no elastic gluten in the rye flour, the gluten it does contain is sticky and does not require kneading. If you are using the additional spices and flavors, then add them now.

Oil and flour a 6½in square pan. Scrape the dough from the bowl into the pan and smooth the top with a spatula. Cover with a cloth and leave in a warm (77°F) place for 5–6 hours, or until doubled in height.

Preheat the oven to 400°F. Oil a sheet of foil and wrap it snugly over the top of the baking pan. Bake for 1½ hours, then carefully remove the foil from the top and bake for an additional hour, so that the upper crust darkens. In Sweden this loaf would traditionally have a charred black crust on top. Allow to cool in the pan. When cold, remove from the pan and wrap well in oiled paper. Leave for two days before eating, as this will make slicing easier.

I wonder if it is the steel gray color that makes us reluctant to embrace rye flour? Across northern Europe, rye is the one bread that is found everywhere, from the expressway truck-stop café to the bread bin in the hillside farmhouse. But in Britain and the US, it is only in the finer restaurants and stores that rye bread is celebrated; what was once the bread of the poor has become the staple of the rich man's table.

TIP The bread's natural tang can be calmed by a shaving of unsalted butter, and together they form a perfect pairing to accompany those other runaway paupers, fresh oysters and smoked eel.

OPPOSITE PAGE, FROM TOP LEFT:
1 Above, rye leaven; below, overnight batter.
2 The mixed dough.
3 The dough scraped into the pan.
4 The risen dough.

Light caraway rye bread

FOR THE FERMENT:
½ cup (125g) water at 68°F (71%)
3 tbsp (50g) sour milk (see tip) (28%)
1 tsp fresh yeast, crumbled (3%)
1½ cups (175g) rye flour (100%)

FOR THE DOUGH:
1 tsp caraway seeds (1%)
½ cup (50g) rye flour (25%)
1 cup (150g) bread flour (75%)
1 tsp fine sea salt (2%)
½ cup (125g) water at 68°F (62%)
¼ tsp fresh yeast, crumbled (0.5%)
1 tsp malt (2.5%)
1 tbsp melted butter (7%)
the ferment (175%)

This bread is similar to those found in the markets in Lviv, in the western Ukraine. I wrote this recipe while baking with the Sisters Meronocyts, at their convent in Ivano-Frankivsk, and it is a faithful reflection of that rye bread. It uses caraway, a traditional ingredient in many rye breads. Caraway is one of the seeds from the parsley family, and was traditionally used both as a flavoring and as a medicinal aid, thought to ease chest and throat infections and to sooth digestion.

TIP The loaf uses sour milk, which I found frequently used in cooking and baking in the Ukraine. On farms, the milk collected from the cow would be poured into plastic mineral water bottles, where it would separate and sour naturally after a few days. Pasteurized milk won't sour, as it lacks the natural bacteria to do this; but a few teaspoons of yogurt or buttermilk, or even lemon juice, stirred into the milk and left to stand for 30 minutes, will give a vague imitation of the souring process.

FOR THE FERMENT Mix together the water and sour milk, then stir in the yeast. Add the rye flour and stir until evenly combined. Cover and leave in a warm (70–77°F) place for 2 hours, until risen and the inner dough is clearly fermenting. To check this is happening, break the surface of the ferment with a spoon: you should see a network of bubbles underneath, and the mixture will have almost doubled in height.

FOR THE DOUGH Preheat the oven to 350°F. On a clean baking sheet, sprinkle the caraway seeds and bake for 10–12 minutes, so they warm and begin to release their fragrance.

Put the flours and salt in a large bowl. In a jug, beat the water with the yeast, malt, and most of the toasted caraway seeds, holding back a few to sprinkle over the top of the loaf. Add the liquid to the ferment, mix lightly but evenly together, then add all this to the flour. Using your hands, mix the dough until it is soft and well combined.

Grease and flour an oblong 3½ x 8in loaf pan. On a lightly oiled (with corn or olive oil) work-surface, tap the dough out into a 10cm square, then roll up into a 4in cylinder that will fit snugly in the pan. Drop it in, seam-side down, then squish it down with your knuckles to flatten the top. Sprinkle the remaining caraway seeds on top, cover and allow to rise for 1½ hours.

Preheat the oven to 425°F. Place the loaf pan in the center of the oven and bake for 30 minutes, then brush the top of the loaf with a little melted butter and continue to bake for an additional 20 minutes, or until the loaf has pulled away from the sides of the pan and the buttered top is a dark shiny brown. Allow to cool on a wire rack. When cool, wrap in waxed paper.

Waterford soda bread

2½ cups (300g) soft whole-wheat flour (100%)
¼ cup (50g) fine oatmeal (17%)
1¼ tbsp lard, dripping, or butter (7%)
1 tsp baking soda (1.5%)
½ tsp fine sea salt (1%)
1 tsp superfine sugar (1.5%)
¾ cup (200g) buttermilk at 68°F (67%)
¾ cup (200g) whole milk at 68°F (67%)
⅓ cup (30g) oatbran (10%)

Michael Power, the baker for Ann Sutton at her bakery in New Ross, Co. Wexford, bakes large squares of tender salty-sweet soda bread in a frame, so that each blob of batter-soft dough spreads and is forced upward. This means the crumb stays tender and moist rather than dry, and the square form of the loaf gives usefully uniform slices. I have adapted his recipe, and added a trick from cake-baking to stop the bread peaking in the middle.

Preheat the oven to 410°F. Grease a deep, 6½in square cake pan with oil or melted butter and dust it liberally with extra wholewheat flour. Tear a sheet of aluminum foil to cover the top of the pan, and leave to one side.

In a large bowl, mix the flour with the oatmeal, then blend in the lard until the lumps have disappeared and the fat is evenly dispersed. Add the baking soda, salt, and sugar, and toss through with your fingers.

In another bowl, combine the buttermilk and milk, then stir this through the flour mixture until you have a thick paste-like dough. Scrape well down to the bottom of the bowl to make sure all of the dry ingredients are mixed evenly through the liquid. Stir quickly: the soda will begin to react with the acid buttermilk as soon as they make contact, and you will need all of the gas produced to lift the loaf.

Sprinkle a little of the oatbran onto the base of the greased and floured pan, then scrape the dough into the pan and sprinkle the rest of the oatbran on top. Pat the dough down lightly so it sits in an even layer. Cover the top of the pan with foil.

Bake for 25 minutes, then remove the foil from the top and bake for an additional 25 minutes. Allow to cool in the pan for a minute, then tip out onto a wire rack. When cool, wrap in waxed paper or freeze in a sealed container.

Denmark

THIS PAGE, TOP TO BOTTOM: geese; a wheaten loaf; Camilla's daughter Asta. OPPOSITE PAGE, CLOCKWISE FROM TOP RIGHT: Camilla Plum; sack of rye grains; farm worker Gitte Knudsen; apples; Per gathering geese; grain labels on the wall of the mill; Karsten Petersen; Bodil's rye bread; OPPOSITE PAGE, CENTER: a farm kitten; Per tasting his home-brew.

There is an air of nobility surrounding a woman who has reached a great age. Bodil Koelster is 76, with a smooth, golden tanned skin and studious lines that frame her calm face. It is late on a cool summer's day when she and her husband William arrive at Fuglebjerggaard, the home and organic farm run by her son Per Koelster and his partner, food writer Camilla Plum. The farm sits upon a slight hilltop in the northern fields of Zealand. Pink-painted outer walls of the old farm buildings face wheat and barley fields and slightly above, on the crest of the hill, graze steers and a few black-faced sheep. Bodil and William have spent the morning at their summer house, where they have picked a basket of ruddy, honey-fleshed mirabelles as a gift for the farm.

On the table sits a freshly baked loaf of rye bread, sharply cornered and dense with moist, plump rye grains, wrapped in an oiled paper bag to protect it as it matures—another gift from Bodil. We sit on old wooden farmhouse chairs gathered around the kitchen table. The sun is hidden behind a sky smooth with a blanket of cloud, lighting the dark wooden surface of the table strewn with coffee cups, bread and butter, and a bowl of freshly-cut flowers from Camilla's garden.

"Most people haven't got the time to bake these days," Bodil says as she unwraps the loaf. "It is perfect," she announces with no regret. "I've worked and tried to perfect the recipe and I think, looking at this loaf, that now it's right. See the bag? This is a tip I've just learned. Brush the loaf with canola oil when it comes out of the oven. Also brush the brown paper bag with oil and, when the loaf is cool, wrap it tightly in the oiled bag. This keeps the loaf sweet and moist." I can smell the distinct aroma of sour rye, and it is indeed a beautiful, remarkable loaf. "When I married I could cook," says Bodil, "and as my mother was a good cook, I had recipes I could adapt from home. It seemed all we could buy at that time was very good bread. All bread was rationed, but at least it was good. You were allocated points to buy bread, but you could convert those to buy flour instead, which many people did. That's what my mother did—she would bake white bread, which you couldn't usually buy. And we'd bake cakes in the pan: plum cakes with raisins and cake spices such as *kummel* (caraway), light in color and sweet; cakes with chocolate studded through them; or citrus cakes. My mother baked until she went to live in a home.

FROM FIELD TO MILL | DENMARK

One of the last things she did, during that last week when she lived in her own house, was to bake a loaf. That was so important to her, and I guess it will be for me too.

"You know, you pick up recipes whenever you get the chance. The recipe for this rye bread was given to me by Per. A young woman he met when he was 25 taught him how to make this loaf, and he taught me," she says, "and in turn my recipe for a sweet yeast bread I used to make at Christmas, that Per loves, I've written down for Camilla."

Camilla Plum is a tall, powerful presence on the farm. She sits across from us at the table subdued from the day's work, the farmer's mountain of daily tasks that reappear as frequently as the rise of the sun. But with a Lutheran zest and respect for work, she rarely loses her humor or passion. Where does her respect for good baking come from? "My mother was the greatest influence on my cooking, and gave me my love of food. I remember in the 1970s she bought a flour mill and experimented with wholewheat bread-making. Those breads," she says and laughs gently, "I got very sick of them. The dough for the wholewheat bread was mixed with a little honey, flour, yeast, water, and salt. This made a soft dough that would be placed in the pan immediately after mixing and then left to rise. During the sixties there was an encouragement by the government to get women into the workforce. In our society women were the keepers of traditions. While women were away the cooking stopped, and industry stepped in to fill the void with supermarkets and prepared foods. We were told the tasks we were used to doing—cooking, looking after children—were worthless.

"Remember, these women were, and still are, the bearers of Danish culture. In Denmark, as in most countries, the complications and demands of cheaper methods of food production affect the qualities of the bread we buy. Customers were persuaded to demand characteristics from these foods that would not naturally be present, as well as a level of convenience that is immodest and at times immoral. We have lost familiarity with how things were made and the association of effort with reward."

The following morning, the workers on the farm gather around this same table, once again spread with coffee cups, bread, sweet butter, and black-currant jelly. Besides Camilla, Per, and their children, there are eight others. Karsten Soenderskov Petersen, 22, is one of them. "I live in my parents' basement," he tells me. "Everybody in my family bakes," he says, almost in surprise when I ask my usual question. I encounter this reaction often here, as baking bread at home is so common that to not bake bread is unusual. "At home we need fresh bread every day, so we take it in turns baking in my parents' kitchen," he says.

Eva Hauch works at the office. We sit in the orchard joking about the proverbs that use bread and baking as a metaphor. "Sometimes when we see a big muscled guy we call him *stort brød* (big bread)," she laughs. Eva asks me when I am leaving. "I'm baking a loaf at the moment," she tells me. "It's still in the oven, but hopefully it will be ready to take out tomorrow." The loaf she is talking about is a dark traditional loaf of *rugbrød* (rye bread). "This *surdej* (sour leaven) comes from Bornholm. Back in Esrum, a friend of our neighbor gave me a small piece of this leaven. They tell me it's over a hundred years old. Many people tell me about these mythical leavens, kept like an heirloom and a part of their heritage. When the children were growing up I would bake with it regularly. Now my friend and I have given pieces of the leaven to other friends, and that sharing is a way of keeping the starter alive, a safeguard to maintain the tradition." She brings the loaf the next morning, carefully wrapped in white waxed paper neatly enclosed at either end with sharp paper folds, and slipped inside a tight clear plastic bag. "Don't eat it today," she warns, "as the crumb will be sticky and clay-like. Leave it for a few days to settle." And I do. It survives the flight without harm, and when I unwrap it on the kitchen table at home it looks perfect. Slightly domed on the upper surface, it has a dark almost chocolatey crust. When sliced, it has a soft waxen texture to the crumb. The flavor is a mixture of the traditional tang of rye, the sourness from the leaven, and a strong aftertaste of licorice.

> "We demand a level of convenience that is immodest.... We have lost familiarity with how things were made and the association of effort with reward."
> —CAMILLA PLUM

Corn bread

I had been lost for an hour, walking around looking for a bakery equipment supplier on the gray outskirts of Turin in Piedmont, when I saw a garage with a coffee bar at the back and nipped inside. And there was this haven. No matter how hard the life of the Italian man, he always has a sensitivity and respect for the finer things in life. As the barman offered to fetch me a cab, I sat in the gentle quietness of this garage café, with a little music, a little espresso, some water, and a small sandwich made with *pane di mais* (corn bread) and layered with *lardo*, fresh basil leaves, and a slice of ripe cold tomato. Here is that yellow bread, both humble and remarkable.

FOR THE POLENTA (makes 5½oz/150g):
1 tsp olive oil
⅓ cup (50g) cornmeal
6 tbsp (100g) water

FOR THE DOUGH
5½oz (150g) polenta (either fresh or leftover) (30%)
1 cup (260g) water at 68°F (52%)
2½ tsp fresh yeast, crumbled (2%)
6 tbsp (100g) buttermilk at 68°F (20%)
1¼ cups (150g) corn flour (30%)
2½ cups (350g) bread flour (70%)
1¼ tsp fine sea salt (2%)

FOR THE POLENTA Take two large dinner plates, oil one with the olive oil and put it to one side. Place the cornmeal in a small saucepan with the water and bring to a boil, stirring constantly until it thickens into a lump that wraps itself to the stirring spoon. Immediately remove the pan from the heat and scrape the cornmeal onto the oiled plate, patting it out flat with the spoon. Cover it with the other plate, up-turned, and allow to cool.

FOR THE DOUGH Thoroughly break up the stiffened polenta in the water, together with the yeast and buttermilk. The easiest way to do this is in a blender, or you could just mash the polenta, yeast, and buttermilk carefully with a fork until you have a smooth paste, then beat the water in a little at a time. The result should be lump-free.

Mix the flours and salt in a bowl and add the polenta paste. Squidge the mixture together until you have a smooth, sticky dough, then leave covered for 5 minutes.

Rub 1 tsp of good olive oil onto the work-surface. Remove the dough from the bowl and place it on the oiled work-surface. Rub a little more oil on your hands, then gently knead the dough for 10 seconds. Round the dough back into a ball, then return to the bowl. Cover with a cloth and leave for 10 minutes.

Knead again on the work-surface for 10 seconds. Round the dough, return to the bowl, cover, and leave for 15 minutes. Keep the kneading quick and even, without breaking the surface of the dough, so that at all times it remains smooth and taut. Repeat the kneading three times at 15-minute intervals, so by the end of 1¼ hours it is smooth, well risen, gently blistered with air bubbles near the surface, and cool to the touch. Leave the dough in a bowl covered with a cloth for an additional 30 minutes.

Rub a clean dishtowel with a handful of flour to stop the dough from sticking, and use it to line a 10in diameter x 4½in deep bowl, or use a linen-lined basket if you have one. Knead the dough gently into a round ball, then place it seam-side-up into the cloth-lined bowl. Gently fold the ends of the cloth back over the top of the dough and allow to rise in a cool place for 1 hour.

Preheat the oven to 425°F. Tip the dough out onto a floured baking sheet and, using a sharp knife, cut a criss-cross pattern in the top of the loaf. Bake for 50–60 minutes, or until the loaf is brown and light in weight.

FROM FIELD TO MILL | CORNMEAL

Crisp cornmeal sticks

The layering of soft folds of dough with butter, fat, or oil, is not unique to puff pastry. The Indian *chapati* gains its flaky texture by being brushed with clarified butter, rolled, then sliced and rolled once more. The pastry for an Italian *sfogliatelle* is rolled ultra-thin, brushed with oil or butter, rolled up into a tube, then sliced thinly and folded around a sweet ricotta filling. In England, the eponymous fat of a lard cake is rolled through the dough to melt during baking. These sticks of bread dough use the same principle. A little onion cooked in butter is mixed with cornmeal and milk, just pushing the flavor over toward something savory.

¼ cup (50g) unsalted butter (17%)
1 cup (110g) finely chopped onion (37%)
½ cup (60g) cornmeal (20%)
1 cup (250g) cold milk (83%)
5oz (140g) white leaven (47%) (see pages 25–27)
¾ tsp fresh yeast, crumbled (2%)
2 cups (300g) bread flour (100%)
1 tsp fine sea salt (2.5%)
12 tsp extra virgin olive oil (20%)
sea salt flakes

Melt the butter in a small saucepan and add the chopped onion. Heat gently over a low flame, with the lid on, for 3–4 minutes, until the onion has softened and become somewhat transparent.

Stir in the cornmeal and cook for 30 seconds. Add 6 tbsp of the milk and stir vigorously for 1 minute until the mixture thickens and comes away from the sides of the pan in a ball. Remove from the heat and tip into a large, cold bowl. Beat in the remaining milk, followed by the white leaven and yeast. Add the flour and salt, then squeeze and stir with your hands until you have a thick, soft dough.

Lightly flour the work-surface and knead the dough for 10 seconds, then cover it with a dishtowel and leave for 5 minutes. Repeat the short kneading, cover the dough, and leave for an additional 5 minutes.

Roll the dough out into a 11 x 14in rectangle. Tip 2 tsp of extra virgin oil onto the dough, then rub or brush the oil so that it covers the surface. Fold the rectangle in by a third at each end. Lift the dough up, dust the work-surface with flour once more, then replace the dough and flour the top. Cover the dough with a dishtowel and leave for 5 minutes to relax.

Repeat the rolling, oiling, folding, and flouring five more times, each time trying to roll the dough to the original dimensions. Remember to leave the dough to rest between rolling, to ensure that it does not tear. Roll the dough once more to 11 x 14in, cover with a dishtowel, and leave for 40 minutes.

Preheat the oven to 425°F. Line a baking sheet with aluminum foil, and rub it lightly with olive oil. Remove the dishtowel, and cut the dough into thin strips that will fit the length of your baking sheet, leaving room for the strips to expand. Sprinkle a few flakes of sea salt down the center of each strip.

Place the tray in the center of the oven and bake for 30 minutes, flipping the sticks over half-way through baking so that they brown evenly. Allow to cool on a wire rack.

You can eat these with thin slices of prosciutto wrapped around them, or use them to dip into a thick soup such as a minestrone.

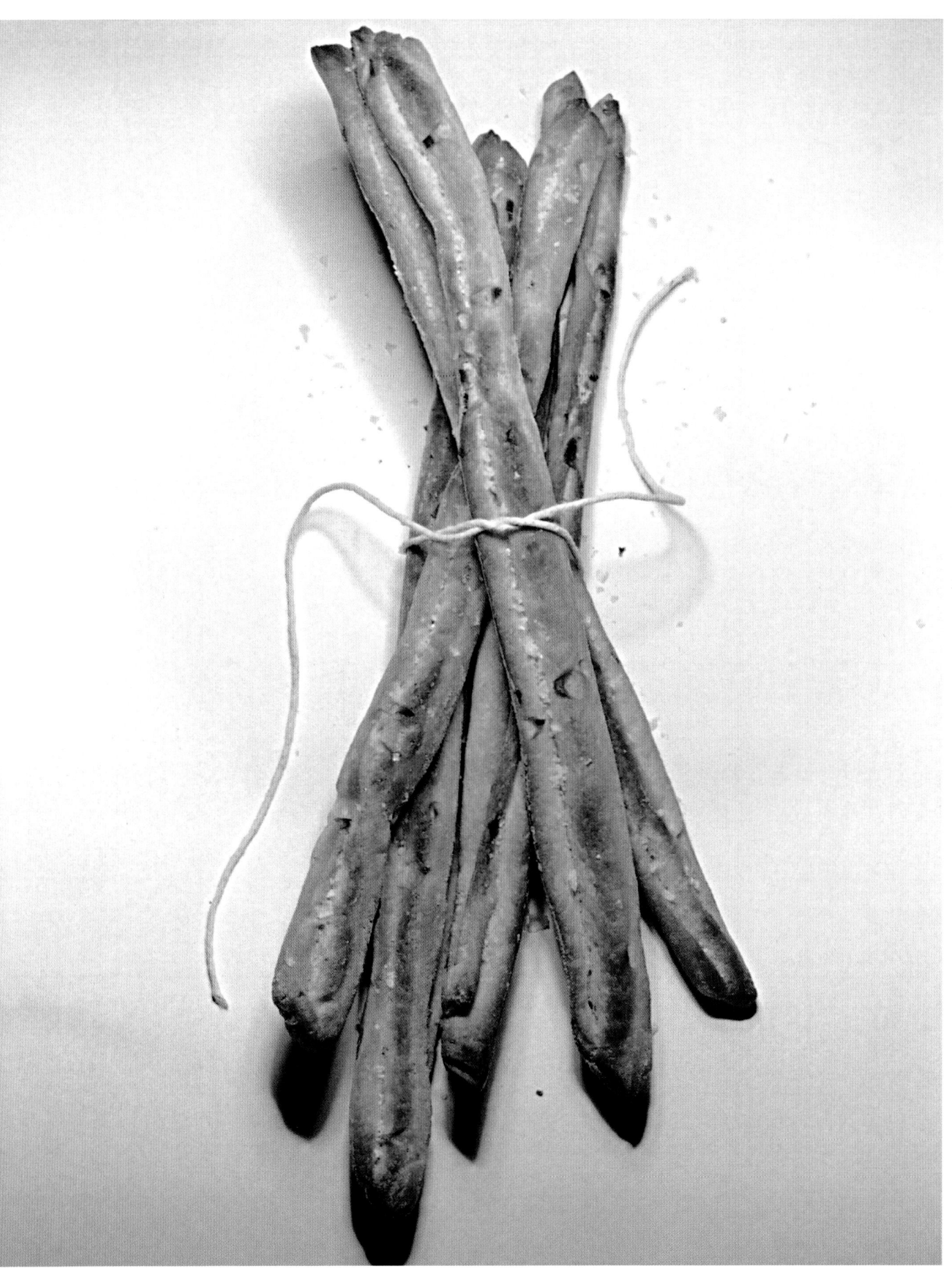

Barley bread

Barley flour, when mixed with water, does not contain the glutinous, elastic protein that will stretch and hold gas inside the loaf. So although it was one of the earliest grains western man relied upon for sustenance, it was quickly left behind when we turned to leavened breads. This recipe uses the traditional flavor of barley in a modern and light-textured loaf.

TIP This recipe attempts to overcome the lack of gluten in barley by using toasted barley flour for flavoring while relying on white flour to keep the loaf light. Cooked whole barley grains are then added to the mixing liquid, held suspended by the gluten in the dough. You could soak these grains in wine, ale, or sour milk to add flavor, but remember to drain them well.

1 scant cup (100g) barley flour (29%)
¾ cup (180g) water at 68°F (52%)
7oz (200g) white leaven (57%) (see pages 25–27)
2½ tbsp honey (14%)
1 tsp fresh yeast, crumbled (1.5%)
1½ cups (240g) cooked barley grains, rinsed until cold (69%)
1¾ cups (250g) bread flour (71%)
1 tsp fine sea salt (2%)

Preheat the oven to 400°F. Spread the barley flour in a thin layer over a baking sheet and bake for 10–12 minutes, until lightly colored.

In a large mixing bowl, stir together the water, leaven, honey, and yeast. When evenly combined, add the barley grains and stir again. Finally, add the toasted barley flour, white flour, and salt, and stir until you have a thick, sticky dough. Tip the dough onto a lightly oiled (with corn or olive oil) work-surface and knead for 10 seconds. Return to the bowl, cover with a dishtowel, and leave for 10 minutes.

Remove from the bowl, knead for 10 seconds, then return to the bowl and leave for 10 minutes. Give the dough a final knead and leave covered in the bowl for 1 hour.

Dust the work-surface with flour. Divide the dough into two equal pieces. Gently knead each piece for 10 seconds and into a ball. Cover and leave for 10 minutes, to give the dough time to relax. Rub a clean dishtowel with flour, so the dough doesn't stick to it, and lay across a large tray (or use long floured baskets).

Sit one ball of dough seam-side-upward on the floured work-surface. To shape the dough (see page 20), pat it flat with your hands, then take the left and right sides furthest from you and fold them inward toward the center by ¼in, making a triangular point. Next, take that same point and fold it inward to the center, pressing it firmly down to seal. Rotate the dough 180°, and repeat with the other side. Rotate the dough once more, so that you are back in the starting position.

If you are right-handed, fold the dough in half toward you starting at the right-hand end, sealing the dough with the heel of your right hand while holding and folding the dough with your left. Roll the shaped loaf (with both hands tucked around it) on the work-surface, pressing down slightly more with the heel of each hand to give the ends a gentle point. Lift the dough and place it seam-side-upward on the cloth. Finally, fold and pull the cloth up the sides of the loaf (or if using a flour-dusted basket, simply place the dough inside it seam-side upward).

Repeat the shaping with the remaining piece of dough and sit this next to the first, separated by the floured cloth. Cover and leave in a warm (70°F) place for 1½ hours. Preheat the oven to 425°F. Turn the dough seam-side-down onto a flour-dusted baking sheet, then apply a fine spray of water. Bake in the center of the oven for 50 minutes, or until the loaf is a light brown in color and light in weight. Cool, then wrap in waxed paper.

Buckwheat pancakes

Buckwheat and oatmeal have a nutty flavor when baked on a griddle as a flatbread. Toast these grains, and this taste is enhanced to become slightly smoky. We often overlook pancakes, but as the first of the noble breads they suit so many of our simpler foods and deserve a closer look. Smoked fish and roe, served with a little sour cream, snipped chives, and melted butter make for a great feast—especially when washed down with a shot of vodka or schnapps.

TIP The whole buckwheat grains soften very rapidly, so they have a delicate texture in the pancakes. Although these flatbreads contain whole grains, each bite is tender and soft.

3 tbsp (50g) boiling water (50%)
⅓ cup (50g) *kasha* (toasted buckwheat) (50%)
½ cup (125g) cold water (125%)
scant ½ tsp fresh yeast, crumbled (2.5%)
1 scant cup (100g) buckwheat flour (100%)
scant ½ tsp fine sea salt (2.5%)
¾ cup (175g) cold milk (175%)
oil, lard, or butter for cooking

Pour the boiling water over the *kasha*, and stir quickly so that the water is evenly absorbed (some kernels will pop open quickly while others will stay crunchy). Pour the cold water over the kernels. Crumble the yeast into the water and stir. Stir in the buckwheat flour until evenly combined, then add the salt and stir again thoroughly.

Cover the bowl and leave in a warm place for 1½ hours, by which time the batter should have risen slightly and a network of bubbles formed under the surface. Stir in the cold milk until you have a thin batter.

Preheat a non-stick skillet, and 1 tsp of oil, lard, or butter. Heat until it is almost smoking hot. The oil is important, even with the non-stick pan, as it helps crisp the edges of the pancakes and adds to their flavor.

Ladle about 3 tbsp batter into the center of the pan and swirl it so that the batter spreads thinly. Replace over the heat, and cook until the edges are crisp and brown and the surface broken with air bubbles—a minute or so. With a spatula, loosen the pancake from the skillet and flip over. Cook for another minute, or until both sides are brown. Remove from the pan, place on a plate and cover with a cloth while you cook the remaining pancakes.

Serve warm with melted butter or sour cream and something like caviar or smoked fish, or as a sweet dish with honey and a squeeze of lemon.

Seeds & grains

Sometimes we let our heads rule our hearts, and it isn't necessarily a good thing. My head imagines that what it likes is always good for me, but my heart needs food that respects my health. The unrefined grain, whole and complete with vitamins, minerals, and fiber, can provide many of the nutrients my body will ever need. Bread-making gets these good grains into an edible package.

F. Marian McNeill's *The Scots Kitchen* describes bound mixtures, for example of fish roe and oatmeal, to make a type of fish "cake." These combine grains into a single form to extend, bulk out, and smooth strong flavors. Dry seeds, rarely palatable, are pleasant once moistened, combined, and cooked like this. The relationship between puddings, loaves, gruel, and stuffing is close; while we like to think of them as separate parts of a meal, the recipes for these foods have one shared goal: to cook grains into a form we enjoy.

The modern diet is about refinement, and the wide availability of refined food was a gift of the industrial age. With nothing brittle, coarse, hard, or tough, everything in our processed food yields easily against our teeth—and usually doesn't require them! Refined, white grainless bread outsells any other sort throughout the world, though we know to live on refined carbohydrate is unhealthy. How do we turn this around? By incorporating wholegrains into the food we eat in a way we like, and by sharing this food with others.

Cooked, soaked wholegrains add a moist heartiness to any bread recipe. You can add up to 20 percent cooked grains to the total flour weight of any bread recipe without needing to alter the other ingredients or quantities. To add more grains, you will need to tweak the recipe as the dough might need more leavening or a change to the water content. Do alter the grains suggested in these recipes to suit your taste or to use what you have available.

MIXED GRAINS | SEEDS AND GRAINS

Five-grain loaf

My first encounter with a good wholegrain rye loaf was in the early 1980s, when I moved to London and stumbled across Neal's Yard, founded by the late Nick Saunders in the 1970s in a visionary move to create a wholefood refuge by the old flower and vegetable market in Covent Garden. The yard was in among old warehouses that kept it separate from the sprawl of the streets around and felt calm and tranquil. At that time I was living and cooking in an ashram in Notting Hill, and would trek there for vegetables and juice. The bakery at Neal's Yard was the home of the sturdy loaf, and this recipe is a nod of respect to those bakers who from the beginning practiced and promoted organic bread-making and the importance of sustainable, responsible living.

1 cup (150g) bread flour (42%)
1 scant cup (100g) whole-wheat bread flour (29%)
1 scant cup (100g) rye flour (29%)
1½ tsp fine sea salt (2%)
7oz (210g) mixed, well-cooked grains (such as rice, lentils, rye or wheat) (60%)
2oz (50g) whole millet (14%)
2½ tbsp oatmeal (9%)
3½oz (100g) white leaven (29%) (see pages 25–27)
2½ tbsp honey (14%)
1 tbsp molasses (7%)
⅔ cup (150g) water at 68°F (43%)
2½ tsp fresh yeast, crumbled (2.5%)
3 tbsp (50g) sunflower oil (14%)
oats or fine oatmeal, for finishing the loaf

In a large bowl, combine the three flours with the salt. In another bowl, mix the cooked grains, millet, and oatmeal with the leaven, honey, molasses, water, yeast, and oil, and beat well until combined. Pour this wet mixture in with the dry ingredients, and stir well until you have a soft, sticky dough. Scrape any dough from your fingers into the bowl, then cover and leave for 10 minutes.

Rub 1 tsp of corn or olive oil on the work-surface and knead the dough on the oiled surface for 10 seconds, ending with the dough in a smooth, round ball. Clean and dry the bowl, then rub lightly with a tsp of oil. Return the dough to the bowl, cover, and leave for an additional 10 minutes. Remove the dough and knead once more on the oiled surface, returning the shape of the dough to a smooth, round ball. Place it back in the bowl, cover, and leave for 1 hour in a warm (70–77°F) place.

Lightly flour the work-surface and shape the dough into a baton (see page 21). Rub a dishtowel with a handful of flour (or use a linen-lined rising basket) and place the dough inside, seam-side-up. Wrap the dough up snugly in the cloth, and allow to rise for 1½ hours, or until almost doubled in height.

Preheat the oven to 410°F. Upturn the loaf onto a flour- or semolina-dusted baking sheet, spray (or brush) the upper surface with water then sprinkle the surface of the loaf with oats or fine oatmeal. Using a sharp blade, slash the loaf diagonally two or three times. Bake in the center of the oven for 30 minutes, then reduce the heat to 375°F and bake for an additional 15–20 minutes until the loaf is a good brown, feels light in weight and sounds hollow when tapped on the base. Allow to cool on a wire rack.

Rolled oat and apple bread

Oats have remarkable properties when combined in breads and give the loaf a chewiness and moistness. If you read the ingredients for processed tray bakes and soft-bite cookies, you'll often see oat flour listed because it can make foods taste richer without the need for so much oil or fat. Here, as with Swiss muesli, the oats are soaked in boiling water then mixed with grated apple. They ensure the bread stays moist and tender over several days.

TIP: Oats vary in quality. When Donnie McLeod cooked porridge for me one morning at his home in Inverness (see page 178), using locally grown organic oats with water and salt, the difference was extraordinary. It had none of that blandness associated with processed breakfast food—instead it had a complex, earthy flavor similar to rye.

½ cup (50g) rolled oats (20%)
6 tbsp (100g) boiling water (40%)
1¼ cups (200g) peeled and grated apple (80%)
3 tbsp (50g) water at 68°F (20%)
3½oz (100g) white leaven (40%)
(see pages 25–27)
¾ tsp fresh yeast, crumbled (2%)
1¾ cups (250g) bread flour (100%)
¾ tsp fine sea salt (2%)
egg wash (see page 187)
oats or fine oatmeal for finishing

Put the rolled oats into a small bowl and pour over the boiling water. Leave aside for 5 minutes while you prepare the other ingredients.

Add the grated apple to the water, leaven, and yeast. Stir the mixture well with a fork so that the yeast dissolves, then stir the soaked oats into this. In another bowl mix the flour with the salt. Pour the wet ingredients into the flour and stir the mixture with your hands until it is evenly combined and you have a soft, sticky dough. Scrape any dough from your fingers into the bowl, then cover and leave for 10 minutes.

Rub 1 tsp of corn or olive oil on the work-surface and knead the dough on the oiled surface for 10 seconds, ending with the dough in a smooth, round ball. Clean and dry the bowl, then rub lightly with a tsp of oil. Return the dough to the bowl, cover, and leave for an additional 10 minutes. Remove the dough and knead once more on the oiled surface, returning the shape of the dough to a smooth, round ball. Put it back in the bowl, cover and leave for 1 hour in a warm (70–77°F) place.

Lightly flour the work-surface and shape the dough into a baton (see page 21). Rub a dishtowel with a handful of flour (or use a linen-lined rising basket) and place the dough inside seam-side-up. Wrap the dough up snugly in the cloth, and allow to rise for 1½ hours, or until almost doubled in height.

Preheat the oven to 410°F. Upturn the loaf onto a flour- or semolina-dusted baking sheet then dust the surface of the loaf with oats or fine oatmeal. Bake the loaf in the center of the oven for 30 minutes, then lower the heat to 375°F and bake for an additional 15–20 minutes, until the loaf is a good brown, feels light in weight, and sounds hollow when tapped on the base. Allow to cool on a wire rack.

Wholegrain rye bread

This loaf is similar to the one baked by Bodil Koelster in Denmark, and typical of the type of wholegrain rye once common in that region. There is a certain grace to this bread, with its clean form unfussed by cuts or tricky ends. It is a simple rye bread, combining wholegrains and light flour with a clean acidic tang given by the hefty dose of leaven. I've added a little yeast, but if you have the time, and if your leaven is bright and active, make it without. You can simply cook and soak the rye grains in water, but I like the taste of a little bottle of real ale used for an overnight marinade.

TIP Like all 100 percent rye breads, leave the loaf for a day (or even two), wrapped tightly in waxed paper, before slicing thinly. I like to serve this rye bread with cured fish and marinated vegetables and, like a good Roquefort, it is helped by a scraping of unsalted butter.

⅔ cup (150g) water at 68°F (60%)
7oz (200g) rye leaven (80%) (see pages 25–27 and 31)
¼ tsp fresh yeast, crumbled (0.5%)
14oz (400g) cooked and soaked rye grains (160%) (see page 49)
¾ tsp fine sea salt (0.5%)
2 cups (250g) light rye flour (100%)

Beat together the water, leaven, and yeast until evenly combined, then stir in the grains. In a larger bowl, mix the salt and rye flour together with your fingers, then pour in the grains and liquid. Squidge the mixture together until you have a very soft, sticky paste of a dough (the dough will be constrained by the sides of the pan). Scrape any dough from your fingers into the bowl, then cover and leave for 10 minutes.

Evenly oil and dust with rye flour an 8 x 4in loaf pan. Scrape the dough from the bowl into the pan, then smooth down the top of the dough so that it sits flat in the pan. As the dough contains no elastic gluten to give it resilience, there is no benefit to giving it a first rise. Simply get it into the pan and let it rise once before baking. Cover the pan and leave the dough for 2½ hours, or until the loaf has risen in height by a third.

Preheat the oven to 410°F. Uncover the pan and prick the upper surface of the dough lightly with a fork. Bake the loaf in the center of the oven for 20 minutes, then reduce the heat to 400°F and bake for an additional 25–30 minutes. By this time the loaf should be a dark golden-brown on the upper surface and the dough should have pulled away slightly from the sides of the pan. Leave the loaf in the pan for 10 minutes to cool slightly. Using a dull knife, carefully ease the loaf out onto a wire rack to finish cooling.

When the loaf is cool, lightly oil a brown paper bag and wrap the bread up snugly inside it. Store the loaf for at least two days, at a cool room temperature, before slicing thinly to serve.

SEEDS AND GRAINS | OATMEAL

Golspie loaf

Sometimes grains can simply form a crust on the loaf. Here, coarse-milled oatmeal lines the pan for a bread made with a soft, moist dough. I wrote this recipe at the historic Golspie watermill up in the Scottish highlands, where an old grain known as bere is still milled and used to make a type of flatbread known as a bere bannock. As wheat was always an important and valuable crop, the poor people would only have the less highly regarded oatmeal and bere barley to use for food. Now wheat has become far more common and ordinary, yet oatmeal and barley have dwindled in popularity except by those who value wholegrains in their diet. By combining the two, with the barley as the leaven and the oatmeal as the crust, a plain wheaten loaf becomes a nutritionally complex and satisfying bread.

1 cup (250g) water at 68°F (62%)
10½oz (300g) barley or rye leaven (75%)
   (see pages 25–27 and 31)
¾ tsp fresh yeast, crumbled (1%)
3⅓ cups (400g) whole-wheat bread flour (100%)
1 tsp fine sea salt (2%)
½ cup (75g) coarse oatmeal, for dusting the loaf (19%)

Beat the water with the leaven and yeast. In a large bowl, toss the whole-wheat flour with the sea salt, then stir in the liquid. Mix this until you have an evenly combined, soft and sticky dough. Scrape any dough from your fingers into the bowl, then cover and leave for 10 minutes.

Rub 1 tsp of corn or olive oil on the work-surface and knead the dough on the oiled surface for 10 seconds, ending with the dough in a smooth, round ball. Clean and dry the bowl, then rub lightly with a tsp of oil. Return the dough to the bowl and leave for an additional 10 minutes. Remove the dough and knead once more on the oiled surface, returning the shape of the dough to a smooth, round ball. Place it back in the bowl, cover, and leave for 1 hour in a warm (70–77°F) place.

Rub an 8in springform cake pan with oil. Sprinkle half the oatmeal evenly around the inside of the pan. Lightly flour the work-surface, and roll the dough into a disc measuring something just short of 8in in diameter. Lift this up and press it into the pan. Using the knuckles of your hand, press the dough into the edges of the pan so that it sits evenly. Dust the upper surface of the dough with additional oatmeal. Cover the surface of the pan loosely with a cloth and leave in a warm (70–77°F) place for 1 hour, or until almost doubled in height.

Preheat the oven to 410°F. Score the dough with a deep cross, right through to the base of the pan. This will allow the bread to be broken into quarters after it has been baked. Bake in the center of the oven for 25 minutes, then reduce the heat to 375°F and bake for an additional 20 minutes, or until the loaf is a dark golden-brown on the upper surface. Remove from the oven, unclasp the pan, and remove the loaf to finish cooling on a wire rack.

Lentil rolls

The dry peppery taste of a lentil is suited to a light, rye-based dough, as the astringency of the rye lightens what might otherwise be a heavy flavor. The lentils are cooked until they are quite soft before being added to the dough so they combine well and bake moistly. Slightly sweet with a tender crumb, these dinner rolls are good with a broth-based soup such as cock-a-leekie or spring vegetable. Freeze them as soon as they're cold, in an airtight container, and reheat in a 350°F oven for 10–12 minutes.

2½ cups (200g) cooked Puy lentils, soft and drained (80%)
6 tbsp (100g) water at 68°F (40%)
1 tsp fresh yeast, crumbled (1.5%)
1½ tbsp honey (10%)
1½ cups (200g) bread flour (80%)
½ cup (50g) rye flour (20%)
¾ tsp fine sea salt (2%)

Beat the cooked lentils with the water, yeast, and honey, and leave to one side. In a large bowl combine the white and rye flours with the salt, then pour the yeast-liquid in. Mix until you have an evenly combined, soft and sticky dough. Scrape any dough from your fingers into the bowl, then cover and leave for 10 minutes.

Rub 1 tsp of corn or olive oil on the work-surface and knead the dough on the oiled surface for 10 seconds, ending with the dough in a smooth, round ball. Clean and dry the bowl, then rub lightly with a tsp of oil. Return the dough to the bowl, cover, and leave for an additional 10 minutes. Remove the dough and knead once more on the oiled surface, returning the shape of the dough to a smooth round ball. Place it back in the bowl, cover, and leave for 1 hour in a warm (70–77°F) place.

Lightly flour the work-surface and roll the dough into a sheet measuring 10 x 8in. Lay this sheet of dough on a tray lined with a flour-dusted cloth, then cover the surface of the dough with another cloth and leave for 1 hour, or until almost doubled in height.

Preheat the oven to 410°F. Uncover the dough and cut into 16 squares. Carefully lift the rolls up and place them on a flour-dusted baking sheet, ensuring that the edges do not touch. Bake in the center of the oven for 25 minutes, or until the tops of the rolls are golden brown and feel light.

Rice bread

Left-over rice, even if it's over-cooked but with the grains still separate, can be mixed into dough to make a sturdy, simple, white loaf. This loaf, which I enjoy toasted in the morning, uses milk and a little honey to slightly sweeten and help color the crumb when toasted. This is important as the rice doesn't take color very quickly.

TIP For the pictures I used an old-fashioned Pullman loaf pan. This has a sliding cover, producing a uniform loaf that gives you square slices. You can buy Pullman pans from specialty kitchen equipment suppliers. But no harm will come if you use an ordinary pan and let the top of the loaf pop up.

1 cup (150g) tender cooked rice (preferably short-grain) (60%)
⅔ cup (150g) milk at 68°F (60%)
1¼ tsp fresh yeast, crumbled (2%)
2 tbsp honey (16%)
1¾ cup (250g) bread flour (100%)
¾ tsp fine sea salt (2%)

In a pitcher or bowl, beat together the rice, milk, yeast, and honey. In a larger bowl, toss the flour and salt between your fingers, then pour the liquid in and mix until you have an evenly combined, soft and sticky dough. Scrape the dough from your fingers into the bowl, cover and leave for 10 minutes.

Rub 1 tsp of corn or olive oil on the work-surface and knead the dough on the oiled surface for 10 seconds, ending with the dough in a smooth, round ball. Clean and dry the bowl, then rub lightly with a tsp of oil. Return the dough to the bowl and leave for an additional 10 minutes. Remove the dough and knead once more on the oiled surface, returning the shape of the dough to a smooth, round ball. Place it back in the bowl, cover, and leave for 1 hour in a warm (70–77°F) place.

Grease the inside of a 4 x 11in Pullman loaf pan with a snug-fitting lid. If you can't get one, then use a slightly smaller pan and allow the dough to rise out of it. Shape the dough into a baton (see page 21), then place it in the pan seam-side-down. Slip the lid over the pan (or cover the dough with a cloth) and leave for 1 hour, or until almost doubled in height (or close to touching the lid).

Preheat the oven to 410°F. If your loaf is in a pan with a lid, simply place in the center of the oven. If your loaf is in an open pan, dust the top with flour, then place it in the oven. Bake for 25 minutes, then reduce the heat to 375°F and bake for an additional 20 minutes, or until the loaf has pulled away slightly from the sides of the pan and is a good golden-brown. Remove from the pan and allow to cool on a wire rack.

Germany

There are foods that remind us, very subtly, of flavors from our childhood. For me a fine bread-crumbed gratin, soft underneath with melting cheese, will always be, somewhere deep in my mind, cheese on toast. Our parents got in early and taught us, with a mixture of love and angst, what they thought was good. They gave us their personal best list—flavors that meant something to them. My father would cook tripe on Saturdays, and now, when I see tripe on a menu, my first thought is "my father would like that."

It is in the home that we get our first opportunity to learn about good food, and sharing a loaf that you have baked can help teach the people who you share your home with. Sharing home-baked bread encourages home-baking.

As often as she can, Julia Decker spends time writing down recipes that have been told to her by her father and grandmother. First she writes them on scraps of paper and post-it notes, then she transcribes them into a hardback book. As with many families, the recipes of Julia's relatives are remembered rather than written down, but having her own hand-written recipe book ensures that methods and techniques will stay close to her parents' and grandparents' intent when they are passed on to her children.

Julia's two-room apartment in Munich is small, with a kitchenette in which she bakes bread. She doesn't bake every day, but rather a few times a year. So she is a "sometime baker," someone who bakes a few times a year because it's a pleasure. Around the world there are lots of just this sort of baker: "sometimers" who dig out an old recipe and bake over a day to see how they fare.

During the 1980s in Germany, the organic and Demeter (an association that encourages farmers to view the soil as a living thing) movements became prominent in food retailing, and bakers who promoted wholegrain breads became popular. The best word to describe the crumb of these loaves is "compact"—they are like a grain terrine studded with moist whole grains of rye, wheat, spelt, or linseed. The grains combine to give flavor and texture, and with other seeds mark the flavor territory that is represented by each baker.

Chains such as the excellent Hopfpfisterei and Fritz-Mühlenbäckerei, as well as independent bakers, who sell at the Viktualien outdoor market, supply remarkable breads rich with seeds and grains without

ABOVE, CLOCKWISE FROM TOP: a street in central Munich; Julia Decker as a child with her father on a donkey in Greece; baker Franz Stricker holds salt-crusted crescent rolls; Stricker's coriander seed bread; OPPOSITE, CLOCKWISE FROM TOP LEFT: wholewheat Demeter bread at the Viktualien market in central Munich; handfuls of soft dough; Stricker holding a typical Bavarian dark rye bread; a loaf from the Hopfpfisterei bakery; spiced *vinschgauer schüttelbrot* from the southern Tyrol; Stricker's lye-dipped and baked pretzels; Stricker's wooden-basket-proved rye bread; Julia compiles her family's recipes; a young Julia, with the blonde hair, makes sandwiches with her school friend Philipp; Julia in her Munich apartment.

Baker Franz Stricker with his oven.

> "At Franz Stricker's store... the old electric oven was built in the 1950s, yet is kept gleaming like a loved car."

even the slightest nod toward white softness. But still these bakeries also sell ingredients for home-baking—sachets of leaven, whole grains, flour, and sea salt—and they promote themselves as centers for baking excellence rather than simply as retailers of their own good loaves.

Prior to this change, finding good bread in Germany was not so easy. "When my brother and I were young," says Julia, "there was no possibility of buying good bread, so my father started to bake bread at home: bread with taste, not like white toast." We knead dough together on the bleached wooden table, and we talk about her father's bread. "It was really good, made with a grain that we call *dinkel*, but that you call spelt, which has a rich nutty taste. It is still the flour I use when I bake.

"There is a famous German cookbook writer, who wrote a book about baking in which he included a recipe inspired by the bread my father used to bake. My surname is Decker, so he called it *deckerspeziellbröt*, which means 'Decker's special bread.' My father always made this kind of bread, and in the early 1980s it was unusual to bake bread at home."

Not all recipes get noted and recorded, though. Sometimes a baker's work is a performance that only remains as a memory after the baker and bread have gone. Walking down Klenzestraße, a tiny side street in the down-town district off the Gärtnerplatz, I notice a stack of unusual rye flatbreads in a window. The bakery is open, and the baker Franz Stricker is there. His little store has a gentle disorder about it, with bags of cookies and cut sandwiches and, behind the counter, racks sparsely lined with the week's last remaining loaves.

Franz invites me to see the ovens, so we exit through the back of the shop into a small courtyard and across to a door on the other side. The door leads to a narrow spiral staircase that decends into the basement where, tucked away at the back of another building, is his bakery. The space is lined with wooden shelves, and from the ceiling hang the peels, brooms, and long scrapers that are the ovenman's tool kit. Light streams in through windows that open out onto a light well, and between these windows is a well-used wooden bench, where scrapers and brushes are kept in a small pot.

Franz explains how some of the other breads are baked. "Here," he says, carefully lifting the lid on a large oblong tray, "is the lye dip for the pretzels, which is the best way to get that dark red color on the crust." Around from that is the old electric oven, built in the 1950s yet kept gleaming like a loved car. He races around, getting other loaves out to photograph, most of which have spices such as coriander, aniseed, or fennel or fragrances such as lemon or orange zest in the rye dough.

Franz explains how the flatbread I'd seen in the window is made. "I toss it between two sheets of board," he says, "back and forward until the constant slapping flattens it." This traditional bread from the southern Tyrol is called *vinschgauer schüttelbrot*. It is almost all crust, and resembles a large savory cracker, being quite crisp and dry. The recipe is unusual, using rye flour, rye leaven, water, salt, and a hefty dose of fennel, anise, and citrus zest.

I ask Franz what will happen to his recipes. "They end here," he says, holding his arms out in the room, "I'm 56, and there is no one to pass the recipes on to. This is where I bake and this is where the recipes will probably stay."

Sunflower bread

This is a very simple quick loaf to make, jam-packed with toasted sunflower seeds and with a slight taste of honey. Toasting the seeds makes them taste almost nut-like.

1½ cups (200g) bread flour (80%)
½ cup (50g) millet flour (20%)
1½ cups (200g) sunflower seeds, lightly toasted (80%)
¾ tsp fine sea salt (2%)
2½ tbsp honey (20%)

3½oz (100g) white leaven (40%)
  (see pages 25–27)
¾ tsp fresh yeast, crumbled (1%)
6 tbsp (100g) water at 68°F (40%)
beaten egg or milk, for glazing
  the loaf prior to baking)

In a large bowl, combine the bread and millet flours with the toasted sunflower seeds and salt. In another bowl or pitcher, beat the leaven with the honey, yeast, and water. Pour the liquid in with the dry ingredients, and stir well until you have an evenly combined, soft and sticky dough. Scrape any dough from your fingers, then cover the bowl and leave for 10 minutes.

Rub 1 tsp of corn or olive oil on the work-surface and knead the dough on the oiled surface for 10 seconds, ending with the dough in a smooth, round ball. Clean and dry the bowl, then rub lightly with a tsp of oil. Return the dough to the bowl and leave for an additional 10 minutes. Remove the dough from the bowl and knead once more on the oiled surface, returning the shape to a smooth, round ball. Place it back in the bowl, cover, and leave for 1 hour in a warm (70–77°F) place.

Lightly flour the work-surface and shape the dough into a ball (see page 21). Rub a dishtowel with a handful of flour and place the dough inside, seam-side-up. Wrap the dough up in the cloth, then place this inside an 8-cup deep, round bowl. This will help force the dough to rise upward rather than spread outward and give height to the dough. Allow it to rise for 1½ hours, or until almost doubled in height.

Preheat the oven to 410°F. Upturn the loaf onto a flour-dusted baking sheet, then brush the loaf with beaten egg. Cut a deep cross in the center of the loaf. Bake in the center of the oven for 30 minutes, then lower the heat to 375°F and bake for an additional 15–20 minutes, until the loaf is a good brown color, feels light in weight, and sounds hollow if tapped on the base. Cool on a wire rack.

Linseed and wheat bread

Linseed (or flax seed, as it is otherwise known) is commonly found in mixed seed breads in Germany. A very important seed in European folk medicine, it was reputed to encourage healing if made into a paste and spread over a wound as a poultice. It contains high levels of alpha-linolenic acid, an essential fatty acid that must form part of our diet if we are to remain alert and healthy. A little linseed each week will only do the body good.

TIP But like all heavy-grain breads, I prefer a little often, so I've shaped this loaf into a stick that cuts into thin, bite-sized discs. Serve with a scraping of butter and a little berry jelly.

1 cup (150g) bread flour (60%)
1 scant cup (100g) whole-wheat bread flour (40%)
¾ tsp fine sea salt (2%)
¾ cup (100g) golden linseed (40%)
2 tsp ground malt powder (5%) (see page 38–39)
⅔ cup (150g) water at 68°F (60%)
1 tsp fresh yeast, crumbled (2%)

In a large bowl, combine the two flours with the salt, linseed, and malt powder. In another bowl or large pitcher, beat the water with the yeast. Pour the liquid in with the dry ingredients, and with your fingers squidge the two together until you have an evenly combined, soft and sticky dough. Scrape any dough from your fingers back into the bowl, cover and leave for 10 minutes.

Rub 1 tsp of corn or olive oil on the work-surface. Knead the dough on the oiled surface for 10 seconds, ending with the dough in a smooth, round ball. Clean and dry the bowl, then rub lightly with a tsp of oil. Return the dough to the bowl and leave for an additional 10 minutes. Remove the dough and knead once more on the oiled surface, returning the shape of the dough to a smooth, round ball. Place it back in the bowl, cover, and leave for 1 hour in a warm (70–77°F) place.

Divide the dough into two even pieces, then shape each into a baton (see page 21). Leave these dough pieces on the work-surface for 10 minutes, covered lightly with a cloth. Roll each one out still further, into a sausage shape 12in long. Place these on a flour-dusted baking sheet, then cover with a cloth and leave for 1 hour, until doubled in height.

Preheat the oven to 410°F. Uncover the dough and brush the upper surface of each stick lightly with water. Bake in the center of the oven for 25 minutes, then reduce the heat to 375°F and bake for an additional 20 minutes, or until the loaves are golden brown and feel light in weight. Allow to cool on a wire rack.

Griddled buckwheat muffins

An English muffin is a twice-cooked bread, baked on the griddle then split and toasted on the fire. The honeycomb texture of a good muffin is suited to runny, dripping foods, such as soft poached eggs with melted butter, or warm hollandaise over wilted spinach. The muffin catches the sloppy stuff, which wets the crisp, toasted surface. As buckwheat cooks quickly and plumps within minutes of being soaked with hot water, it is well suited to a soft dough like this.

TIP If you want the muffins to toast quickly, try adding a little sugar to the dough, either in the form of honey or syrup (1 tbsp is enough), or replace half the water with milk. This will make sure they color extra quick and stay soft. I prefer a crunchier toasted muffin so I leave the sweetening out.

6 tbsp (100g) boiling water (29%)
½ cup (75g) toasted buckwheat (22%)
2 tbsp cider vinegar (9%)
2½ cups (350g) bread flour (100%)

1 tsp fine sea salt (2%)
¾ cup (200g) water at 68°F (57%)
¾ tsp fresh yeast, crumbled (1.5%)
2 tbsp melted butter (7%)

Pour the boiling water over the buckwheat, then add the cider vinegar and stir. Leave for 5 minutes for the buckwheat to slightly swell and absorb the water.

In a large bowl, combine the flour and salt. In another bowl, stir the soaked buckwheat with the water and yeast, then add this to the flour. Mix the dough together quickly and evenly until you have a soft, sticky mixture. Next, pour over the warm melted butter and work this evenly into the dough. Scrape any dough from your fingers into the bowl, then cover and leave for 10 minutes.

Rub 1 tsp of corn or olive oil on the work-surface and knead the dough on the oiled surface for 10 seconds, ending up with a smooth, round ball. Clean and dry the bowl, then rub lightly with a tsp of oil. Return the dough to the bowl and leave for an additional 10 minutes. Knead the dough once more on the oiled surface, returning it to a smooth round ball. Return the dough to the bowl, cover, and leave for 1 hour in a warm (70–77°F) place.

Lightly flour the work-surface, then roll the dough out into a 10 x 8in rectangle about ¼in thick. Using a round 4in cutter, cut discs from the dough and lay them on a flour-dusted tray or cloth. Continue with the remainder of the dough, re-rolling any scraps and cutting more to finish. Cover the muffins with a cloth and leave in a warm (68–77°F) place for 45 minutes to rise.

Take a large skillet, ideally one with a close-fitting lid. Shake a little extra flour lightly over the muffins then, using a spatula, carefully transfer the muffins to the dry pan, three or four at a time. Cover the pan and leave over a gentle heat for 5 minutes, peeking underneath the muffins after a few minutes to see if the heat needs to be turned up or down. The trick is to let them cook for 5 minutes per side, adjusting the heat accordingly. If you cook them for too short a time, the muffins will be doughy and uncooked in the middle; too long a time, and the muffins will be dry. Once one side is cooked, carefully flip them over and cook on the other side. When they're done, remove and cool on a wire rack, then continue to cook the remaining muffins. When they're cold, store in a paper bag or freeze.

Abundant harvest

There is a small apple tree in a large pot in our garden, rescued from under the shade of a grapevine. It was stunted from lack of sunlight, so I dug it up and put it in the pot so it could be moved around the garden to follow the sun. The tree is a James Grieve, an English variety popular in the late 19th century for its sweet juice and fragrance. For a few years, the tree budded with pink blossoms which dropped off without fruiting. But after the third year, two small apples appeared, and I watched their progress daily, brushing off the greenfly and stopping the cats from biffing them. After a burst of late summer rain, one fell off green and hard; the other withered under an attack from wasps.

Down the road, by Merton Abbey mills where William Morris printed fabric, many old apple trees grow in the gardens of the houses that surround the supermarket plonked on the site of the medieval priory. There were once orchards, but now only these trees in people's gardens remain. Last summer, I walked by the stream to the mill and on the wall outside one house was a bag of apples next to a sign that read: "Please take—for free." Each day I walked there, those same apples sat untouched while the supermarket heaved with bag-laden carts. No one took the apples. Eventually, they shriveled.

Every year, mature fruit trees produce an abundance of ripe apples, with one tree producing more than one family can use. What can you do with this free fruit? Juice some, make pies with a butter-rich crust, brew a simple scrumpy, peel and cook them long and slow until only a dark concentrate remains, sun-dry even more to use during the winter months. You might use apple flesh to stud a simple dough, and mix the juice with the leavening. Whatever you have an excess of, make it useful and a blessing. Use the fruit of the harvest in every possible way: this is kitchen economy and good living.

Spotted soda bread

Sometimes called spotted dick, this plain cake-like loaf is sold in the south of Ireland and, when fresh, has a creamy taste and a slight sweetness to the crumb. Though the crust is quite crisp for the first couple of hours after baking, it soon settles to something softer, like a fruit cake crust. This recipe contradicts the generosity of others in this chapter, as the currants are there to "spot" the bread, reflecting its frugal origins. Adding more fruit is simply not done. Well, not in a normal home, as my mother would say. Choose to add more at your peril.

TIP Eat this in slices as you would a scone—freshly baked with a little butter and a good preserve.

2½ cups (300g) all-purpose flour (100%)
½ tsp sea salt (1%)
2 tsp baking powder (3%)
¼ cup (50g) butter (17%)
1 cup (250g) milk at 68°F (84%)
2½ tbsp corn syrup (17%)
⅓ cup (50g) currants or golden raisins (17%)

Oil and flour the inside of a 4½ x 7in oblong pan. Preheat the oven to 410°F.

In a large bowl, combine the flour, salt, and baking powder, then rub in the butter until the mixture resembles fine bread crumbs. In another bowl or a pitcher, beat the milk with the corn syrup until combined. Drop the currants or golden raisins into this to wet them, then pour the liquid mixture into the dry ingredients and mix. Scrape the batter into the prepared pan.

Smooth the top of the batter down lightly with a spatula, and loosely cover the top of the pan with foil. Bake in the center of the oven for 20 minutes, then remove the foil and bake for an additional 20 minutes, or until the top of the bread is a good golden-brown. Remove from the oven, leave for a few minutes to cool and firm, then carefully remove the bread from the pan and allow to cool on a wire rack.

Raisin and cinnamon loaf

Fruited bread should be just that: bread so thick with rich, plump fruit that some inevitably breaks through the outer surface of the dough, no matter how carefully it is shaped. There are bakers who would reduce the amount of fruit to preserve the appearance but they, luckily, don't have to eat what they make. The complaint I frequently hear from customers is that the fruit and nut breads they buy seem mean. Now, although bakers must struggle to make a bread that doesn't punish their profits, this dilemma shouldn't affect the home baker. Produce the food you want to make, exactly the way you want to eat it.

TIP I can hear the voice of one baker I used to work with saying, "What? 50% raisins! Far too much!" Percentages explain how to achieve the best results. If you only have a few raisins, halve the other ingredients and make a smaller loaf.

OPPOSITE PAGE, FROM TOP LEFT:
1 The shaped loaf
2 The risen loaf on the tray.
3 The baked loaf.
4 The sliced loaf.

2 cups (300g) bread flour (75%)
⅔ cup (75g) rye flour (19%)
¼ cup (25g) whole-wheat flour (6%)
1 tsp fine sea salt (2%)
½ tsp ground cinnamon (0.5%)
5½oz (150g) rye leaven (38%)
 (see pages 25–27 and 31)
¾ cup (175g) water at 68°F (43%)
3 tbsp (50g) olive oil (13%)
1 tsp fresh yeast, crumbled (1%)
1 tbsp honey (6%)
1⅓ cups (200g) raisins (50%)

Combine the three flours with the salt and cinnamon. In another bowl, beat the leaven, water, olive oil, and yeast with the honey and raisins (I add the raisins to the liquid as the moisture helps the dough stick to them—some recipes suggest adding them later, but this only really applies to aggressive machine-mixing; hand-mixing is gentle and will not tear the fruit). Combine the wet mixture with the dry ingredients and stir with your hands to make an evenly combined dough. Scrape any dough from your fingers into the bowl, cover, and leave for 10 minutes.

Rub 1 tsp of corn or olive oil on the work-surface and knead the dough on the oiled surface for 10 seconds, ending with the dough in a smooth, round ball. Clean and dry the bowl, then rub lightly with a tsp of oil. Return the dough to the bowl and leave for an additional 10 minutes. Remove the dough and knead once more on the oiled surface, returning the shape of the dough to a smooth, round ball. Place it back in the bowl, cover, and leave for 1 hour in a warm (70–77°F) place.

Lightly flour the work-surface and gently knead and shape the dough into a ball (see page 21). Using your fingers or your elbow (the baker's traditional method), dig down into the dough to make a hole through the center. Then work the dough outward with your hands until you have a large ring. Place this on a dishtowel that has been dusted with rye flour and laid across a dinner plate. Pluck the towel through the hole and pull it up a little to stop the loaf from closing in too much. Cover the dough ring with another dishtowel, and leave in a warm (70–77°F) place for 2 hours, or until doubled in height.

Preheat the oven to 410°F. Upturn the dough onto a semolina-dusted baking sheet, peeling off the cloth so that the ring of dough sits bare. Using a sharp scalpel, cut around the circumference of the dough near the top of the loaf, making an incision about ¼in deep. Lightly spray the surface of the loaf with a mist of water, then bake in the center of the oven for 50 minutes, or until the loaf is a good dark brown and feels relatively light in weight. Allow to cool on a wire rack.

1 2
3 4

Fruited barm cake

Though this fruit loaf can be made with a yeasted dough or any simple plain bread dough, I prefer it made with a barm-leavened dough. This adds a dark maltiness, which is often imitated in chemically-leavened recipes by soaking the fruit in ale or tea. Though that can produce a beautiful result, this recipe both teaches you how to add ingredients to a kneaded dough and produces a slightly different, traditional result, with a bread-like, rather than cake-like, texture.

1lb 2oz (500g) dough (from page 41) (100%)
¼ cup (50g) unsalted butter, very soft but not melted (10%)
1 medium egg (12%)
½ cup (50g) all-purpose flour (10%)
¼ cup (50g) dark brown sugar (10%)
⅓ cup (50g) currants (10%)
⅓ cup (50g) golden raisins (10%)
zest of ½ orange (2%)
½ tsp fine sea salt (0.5%)

After the dough has been mixed and briefly kneaded (lightly, three times during the first 30 minutes), return it to the bowl. Add the soft butter—this is a time when you do not want to be disturbed; your hands will be very sticky. Squidging the dough through your fingers in a clenching motion, work the butter into the dough, breaking the dough gently so the butter is forced into it. Beat the egg and add this to the dough. Work the dough again with your fingers until it is almost combined but still somewhat rough.

Mix the flour, sugar, dried fruit, orange zest, and salt, then tip this onto the dough. Work the dough until it is evenly combined. Scrape any dough from your fingers into the bowl, cover and leave for 10 minutes. Give the dough two more light kneads, each 10 minutes apart, on an olive-oiled surface, then cover the dough in the bowl and allow to rise for 2 hours.

Oil and flour a 7in square loaf pan. Shape the dough into a ball (see page 21) and press this seam-side-down into the pan with your knuckles so that it sits flat and even. Cover the pan with a cloth and allow the dough to rise in a warm (77°F) place for 4 hours, or until the loaf has doubled in height.

Preheat the oven to 400°F. Uncover the loaf and bake in the center of the oven for 20 minutes, then lower the heat to 350°F and bake for an additional 20 minutes, covering the top of the loaf with foil toward the end of baking if the loaf looks dark. Remove the pan from the oven, allow to cool and firm for a minute, then carefully remove the loaf from the pan and allow to cool on a wire rack.

Prune and rye babas with Armagnac syrup

Don't think that bread must always precede a meal; it can create the finale. These little prune babas are a dessert bread for when the pudding follows something light and refreshing, such as grilled fish, tender young lettuce, and a fresh tomato salad. At the Relais Plaza, a beautiful restaurant placed on the corner of the Hotel Plaza Athénée, pâtissier Nicolas Berger serves a perfect plain baba, split in a silver bowl, just barely warm and drenched in syrup. Next to it sits another silver bowl filled with the softest whipped cream flavored with vanilla and flecked with the odd brown scrape from the pod. Between the two sits a tiny porcelain pitcher of dark rum. You combine the three as you wish.

TIP This recipe will make 12 babas, and may exhaust your molds. The best solution is to use some of the dough to make a *pain aux pruneaux* in a loaf pan, in addition to babas, and either freeze this after baking or use it in a dessert.

A prune is nothing other than a dried ripe plum, though as a child I was convinced the droopy black skin contained a certain horror. Now, I savor a good prune and its concentrated flavor. Look for soft, moist prunes and use them just as they are.

FOR THE SYRUP:
1 cup (250g) superfine sugar
2 cups (500g) water

FOR THE BABAS:
1½ cups (200g) bread flour (80%)
½ cup (50g) light rye flour (20%)
¾ tsp fine sea salt (2%)
3oz (80g) rye leaven (32%)
 (see pages 25–27 and 31)
6 tbsp (100g) milk at 68°F (40%)
3 medium egg yolks (36%)
¼ cup (60g) superfine sugar (24%)
2½ tsp fresh yeast, crumbled (6%)
½ cup (100g) unsalted butter, softened (40%)
1 cup (200g) soft prunes, pitted (80%)

FOR SERVING:
1 measure of Armagnac for each baba
heavy cream, whipped to soft peaks

FOR THE SYRUP Bring the sugar and water to a boil. Remove from the heat and allow to cool.

FOR THE BABAS In a large bowl, combine the bread flour, rye flour, and salt. In another bowl, beat together the rye leaven, milk, egg yolks, sugar, and yeast. Pour the wet ingredients into the dry and mix until you have a soft, sticky dough. Scrape any dough from your fingers, cover with a cloth and leave for 10 minutes.

Slice the butter into thin pieces and allow to soften. Spread these on top of the dough and work them roughly into it. Tip the dough out onto the work-surface and work it gently and evenly for 5 minutes, until the butter is combined and the dough is smooth. The buttery dough will be quite sticky, but don't worry. Scrape the dough up and place in the refrigerator in a tightly covered large container that allows the dough enough room to rise slowly overnight.

The next day, cut the prunes into quarters. Lightly flour the work-surface and roll out the dough until it measures 12 x 20in. Lay the prunes evenly over two-thirds of the dough, then fold the dough in by thirds. With a rolling pin, knock the dough flat, then fold it in by thirds again. Tap the dough with the rolling pin to seal it, then put back in the bowl and refrigerate for 1 hour.

Lightly grease and flour 12 baba molds. Roll out the dough until it is ⅜in thick and cut it into 2in squares. For each piece, pinch the corners of the dough together to seal them, creating a ball of dough and avoiding getting air pockets trapped in the center. Flip the ball over and press into the prepared mold. Cover with a cloth and allow to rise in a warm (77°F) place for 2 hours, or until doubled in height.

Preheat the oven to 400°F. Place the babas on a baking sheet and bake in the center of the oven for 15 minutes, then reduce the heat to 350°F and bake for an additional 20 minutes, or until the babas are a good brown color. Leave to settle in their molds for a minute, then ease the babas carefully from the molds with a knife.

Serve warm, split open lengthwise, with the syrup spooned over them, together with a little cream and Armagnac. A baba is best left to slightly stale, as it will hold its shape better when later soaked in syrup.

Cherry, fennel, and rye loaf

The cherry used to be an important tree in small communities. Not only were dyes made from the bark and roots, but the thick resin could be chewed as a gum to soothe the throat. The beautiful wood could be fashioned into tables and chairs. And the fruit—well, you already know their rich, tart flavor. At www.treesforlife.org.uk, a charity dedicated to preserving the Caledonian forests, the writer Paul Kendall describes how the wild gaen tree, a type of cherry, had a mysterious place in highland folklore: "...to encounter one was considered auspicious and fateful." In this loaf, a lot of dried cherries are mixed with fennel and rye in the dough and combined with whole rye grains that have been cooked and soaked overnight. It is good sliced and served with soft cheese, liver sausage, and pickles.

TIP A little cherry brandy, or even Swedish cherry wine, can be used to soak the grains overnight.

1 cup (150g) bread flour (60%)
1 scant cup (100g) fine rye flour (40%)
¾ tsp fine sea salt (2%)
2 tsp fennel seeds (4%)
3½oz (100g) rye leaven (40%)
   (see pages 25–27 and 31)
½ cup (125g) water at 68°F (50%)
¼ tsp fresh yeast, crumbled (1%)
1 cup (125g) dried cherries, pitted (50%)
3½oz (100g) cooked and soaked rye grains (40%) (see page 49)
white poppy seeds for dusting

In a large bowl, combine the white and rye flours with the salt and fennel. In another bowl, beat the leaven with the water and yeast, then stir in the cherries and rye grains. Pour this mixture into the dry ingredients, and squidge everything together with your hands until you have a soft, evenly combined dough. Scrape any dough from your fingers into the bowl, cover and leave for 10 minutes.

Rub 1 tsp of corn or olive oil on the work-surface and knead the dough on the oiled surface for 10 seconds, ending with a smooth, round ball. Clean and dry the bowl, then rub lightly with a tsp of oil. Leave the dough in the bowl, covered, for an additional 10 minutes. Remove the dough, knead once more on the oiled surface, returning the shape of the dough to a smooth, round ball. Return it to the bowl, cover, and leave for 1 hour in a warm (70–77°) place.

Lightly flour the work-surface. Remove the dough from the bowl and form it into a baton (see page 21). Lay it on a semolina-dusted baking sheet to rise for 1½ hours, covered loosely with a cloth.

Preheat the oven to 425°F. Uncover the dough and spray the top of the loaf lightly with water. Sprinkle the top of the loaf with poppy seeds then make a cut along the length of the loaf. Bake in the center of the oven for 25 minutes, then reduce the heat to 400°F and bake for an additional 20 minutes, or until the bread is a good dark brown color and feels light in weight. Allow to cool on a wire rack.

This recipe is also good for making two smaller loaves, perhaps one for immediate use and the other for freezing. Simply divide the dough into two equal parts, form each into a baton, then proceed with the rising and baking as described above.

Ireland

Flying back from Ireland, I sat in the departure lounge next to a young man who was returning to England to visit relatives. He told me how his father had left his city career years before and found a piece of land on a hill by a river, where he built his own house. He'd carried and mortared every brick, having dug the foundations by himself with a spade, and then placed every tile on the roof with his bare hands. He plows and thoughtfully farms his land, keeping it organic and sustainable, and tends a garden filled with vegetables and fruit trees, as well as keeping chickens, goats, and pigs. When the young man asked me where I'd been, I said I'd been staying with William Sutherland and Angela Ashe, at the School for Sustainable Living in Killowen. "You've been there?" he gasped, a touch awestruck. "They are my father's heroes."

To explain about the school, I must tell you about its founder, John Seymour. A 20th-century hero, Seymour is a passionate campaigner and activist for a way of life that is respectful of the land and of others, and his actions and battles place him far above the words of many of his contemporaries and allies. He believed, with extraordinary foresight, many years ago, that all was not well as we happily ravaged and consumed the Nature that is around us. He saw that unless we changed our way of life the consequences for this earth would be devastating. Decades later, we now know that Seymour was right.

The school is on a farm that was built by John, William, and Angela, situated up above the banks of the River Barrow, a mile down a long dirt track. It is a small, simple home, and it is against the family background of their children's daily life that lessons are taught, old ways explained, and home-keeping methods practiced.

Baking bread is essential to this family life, and they make a wholegrain soda bread with a moist sturdy crumb. As William measures the ingredients and places them in an earthenware bowl, he explains the reaction of the students to a life devoid of processed foods. "They're surprised by the fussiness," he says. "Food is a living, biological thing, and whether you are growing crops or baking bread, each step you take should be considered and thoughtful."

Into the bowl go oats, whole-wheat flour, eggs, and milk, to be mixed into a paste that resembles thick granola. "We make cider from our own apples," William says, scraping

THIS PAGE, TOP TO BOTTOM: beating eggs for soda bread; the view over Wexford from Slieve Coillte in the John F. Kennedy memorial park; the woodhut in William and Angela's garden. OPPOSITE, CLOCKWISE FROM TOP LEFT: rolled oats and flour; the bowl scraped clean; soda bread; wrapped halves of bread at The Bakehouse; baker Michael Power holding spotted soda bread; loaves and potatoes baking in William Sutherland's Stanley stove; swiss chard after the frost; soda bread dough being scooped into the pan. CENTER: William Sutherland, his dog, and his soda bread.

LEFT TO RIGHT: across the river Barrow at New Ross; William Sutherland's baked soda bread and potatoes.

"Michael Power's... dough, made with whole-wheat flour, buttermilk, soda, salt, and sugar, is so soft that it is almost like a batter."

the dough into oblong loaf pans. "We put a cultured yeast in with the juice and get a reliable cider. It's wonderful how you put this murky brown liquid in and out comes this golden, crystal-clear, fermented cider. But again, because people are used to the filtered, pasteurized stuff, they come in and shake the bottle, which disturbs the layer of natural sediment at the bottom, so then we have to lay the bottle down and leave it to rest and settle again." The bread pans are placed in the Stanley stove together with a few scrubbed potatoes for our lunch, making use of the heat to cook them both simultaneously.

In New Ross, the bright yellow painted Bakehouse bakery sits up on North Street, a gentle slope through the center of the town. New Ross is an old port town, but now only relics such as the towering flour silos from an old mill give a hint to its industrial past. Its warehouses now contain apartments. There is a replica of the SS *Dunbrody* in the harbor, the ship that took immigrants to America, and the town is now a destination for tourists returning to John F. Kennedy's great-grandfather's birthplace in nearby Dunganston. Ann Sutton, the owner of The Bakehouse, shows me the working area of the bakery. An oven, an old upright mixer, a stainless-steel table and wooden baking frames are the core of the bread-baking. Cakes, tarts, small pies, and rich dark fruit cakes help the trade along.

The following morning, baker Michael Power teaches me the knack of soda bread baking, his way. His dough, made with whole-wheat flour, buttermilk, soda, salt, and sugar, is so soft that it is almost like a batter. He dredges the tabletop with flour, then scoops mounds of this dough onto it, tossing it through the flour to coat the outside and round it gently. Then he tucks each piece into the wooden frame, two across by four down. Each piece gently flows as Michael shapes the other pieces, and by the time the tray is filled they just barely touch one another.

Then the tray goes into a hot oven for a short bake, where the loaves rise and fill the corners of the frame. This method produces a loaf and crumb superior to that of the usual dough mixed tightly simply to produce a taut clover shape. He works quickly, as the soda reacts as soon as the buttermilk is mixed with it, and my camera struggles to catch his hands as they speed through the shaping.

That evening, William takes me out to drink Guinness in an old drinking house down on the Hook Head peninsula. The loud singing can be heard from the yard outside, and in the smoky warmth from the peat-fueled fire, we hear songs lamenting love lost, and hard-fought ancient battles against the English, which still bring sadness to the men sat there.

There is a sweet friendliness from the people around me, who are quick to be personal and familiar. I ask William if this is usual. "It's a community built on people helping one another. If someone's car breaks down outside our house, in a way we are really pleased because then, by helping them, we have built up a little bit of credit. So that when we find we need help, they'll be there."

Walnut bread

When making a loaf incorporating nuts or other expensive flavorings, it was once thought sufficient to simply throw scant handfuls of one additional ingredient into the house dough. Not many bakers do that any more. Instead it is usual to layer the flavors through the recipe using different sources. This recipe for walnut bread includes a paste made with walnuts as well as halved walnuts added to the dough. This creates a more complex series of flavors that combine to make a rich, aromatic loaf. This is a bread which I prefer sliced and toasted, spread with a little butter and eaten on its own.

TIP Use good-quality walnuts, ideally the pale sweet ones rather than the darker nuts that seem to taste a little bitter.

Any leftover walnut paste can be eaten as a relish, spread thinly on toast to accompany a slice of mature Cheddar cheese.

FOR THE WALNUT PASTE (makes 3½oz/100g):
- ½ cup (50g) walnuts
- 50g water
- 2 tbsp honey
- 1½ tbsp melted butter, lightly browned
- a pinch of fine sea salt

FOR THE DOUGH:
- 1 cup (220g) water at 68°F (44%)
- 3½oz (100g) rye leaven (20%) (see pages 25–27 and 31)
- 1¼ tsp fresh yeast, crumbled (1%)
- 3½oz (100g) walnut paste (20%) (see left)
- 1 cup (100g) halved walnuts (20%)
- 2¾ cups (350g) all-purpose flour (70%)
- 1 scant cup (100g) rye flour (20%)
- ½ cup (50g) whole-wheat flour (10%)
- 1½ tsp fine sea salt (2%)

FOR THE WALNUT PASTE Place the walnuts, water, honey, browned butter, and salt in the bowl of a small electric spice or coffee grinder. Grind for a few moments until you have a soft, smooth paste.

FOR THE DOUGH Beat together the water, rye leaven, and yeast, and then beat in the walnut paste and fold in the walnut halves. In a second bowl, mix the three flours and the salt, then pour the liquid in with the dry ingredients and combine the dough as evenly as possible, squidging the mixture together with your fingers. Scrape any dough from your fingers into the bowl, cover and leave for 10 minutes.

Rub 1 tsp of corn or olive oil on the work-surface and knead the dough on the oiled surface for 10 seconds, ending with the dough in a smooth, round ball. Clean and dry the bowl, then rub lightly with a tsp of oil. Return the dough to the bowl and leave for an additional 10 minutes. Remove the dough, knead once more on the oiled surface, returning the shape of the dough to a smooth, round ball. Place it back in the bowl, cover, and leave for 1 hour in a warm (70–77°F) place.

Take two dry dishtowels and line two 6-cup deep bowls with them so that the excess cloth hangs over the edge. Dust the cloths liberally and evenly with flour. Divide the dough into two pieces. Round each piece of dough into a ball and place each ball seam-side-up in the cloth-lined bowls. Cover the dough with the edges of the cloth and allow to rise in a warm place for 2–2½ hours, or until almost doubled in height.

Preheat the oven to 410°F. Carefully upturn the dough out onto a flour-dusted baking sheet, and cut a criss-cross pattern in the top. Bake in the center of the oven for 50–60 minutes, until the loaf is a good rich brown color and, when tapped on the bottom, sounds hollow. Allow to cool on a wire rack.

Cobnut loaf with honey and grains

The cobnuts that grow in Kent are a relative of the hazelnut. They first appear covered in a furry green hood that splits at the edges like a medieval trim. Though only occasionally seen in supermarkets, they are easily obtainable by mail order through sites on the internet. At Allens Farm in Sevenoaks, Jill Webb's family picks both the young green nuts from their 100-year-old trees, and later the tree-ripened cobnuts, which taste of oak and coconut. The green nuts are available from late August for four weeks, and the ripe cobnuts after that. Even the windfall nuts are collected and stored in barrels to keep the kernels sweet-tasting and moist. I have a handful of last year's windfall crop, which arrived this morning by mail, sitting shelled in a bowl, and their texture is still crisp and the flavor perfect. Raw kernels have a beautiful, fresh taste; once baked that changes to the familiar toasted flavor we know from nuts in chocolates and cookies.

1 cup (150g) bread flour (30%)
1½ cups (200g) soft all-purpose flour (40%)
1 cup (150g) whole-wheat bread flour (30%)
1¼ cups (300g) water at 68°F (60%)
1¼ tsp fresh yeast, crumbled (1%)
2½ tbsp honey (10%)
1lb (450g) white leaven (90%) (see pages 25–27)
1½ cups (185g) toasted and chopped cobnuts or hazelnuts (37%)
7oz (200g) soaked rye grains (40%) (see page 49)
1½ tsp fine sea salt (2%)
¼ cup (50g) butter, softened (10%)

Combine the flours lightly and leave to one side. In another bowl, put the water, fresh yeast, and honey. Stir well and allow to sit for 10 minutes.

Add the leaven (broken into small pieces), cobnuts, and soaked grains to the liquid. Stir this liquid into the dry ingredients. Mix the mass together well with your hands, squeezing it through your fingertips. When roughly combined, cover the bowl and leave for 10 minutes.

Tip the dough out onto a lightly floured work-surface, sprinkle with the salt, and dot with the softened butter. Knead the dough gently for 2–3 minutes until everything is combined. Return the dough to the bowl, leave for 30 minutes, then knead once more for an additional 2–3 minutes.

Tip the dough out onto a floured work-surface, and give it a turn (see page 21). Leave the dough for an additional 30 minutes, then give it one final turn (as above). Cover the dough and leave for 30 minutes. By now the dough will have rested for 1½ hours.

Divide the dough into two pieces, each roughly 1lb 14oz (875g) in weight. On a lightly floured work-surface, roll each piece out into a circle measuring 8in in diameter. Using a knife, and cutting into the center from the outside of the loaf, make five incisions deep to create the shape shown in the picture (right). Stretch each of these segments by pulling them outward slightly. Sit each piece of dough on a flour-dusted tray, then lightly cover them with a cloth and allow to rise for 1 hour.

Preheat the oven to 410°F. Bake in the center of the oven for 40–50 minutes, until the loaf is a good rich brown in color and, when tapped on the bottom, sounds hollow. Allow to cool on a wire rack.

Sweet chestnut and hazelnut bread

Chestnut flour is a little difficult to work with, producing a crumbly, dry dough if used on its own. Yet when combined with a large proportion of wheat flour, it gives a subtle flavor and tint to the crumb of the loaf. The sweet, earthy taste can be smoothed by adding fat to the dough, here by using butter and fresh cream, and enhanced by pairing it with hazelnuts. At Locanda Locatelli, we christened this bread *pane di brughiera*, the "*brughiera*" being the land where the pasture meets the woods.

It is appropriate for a bread that combines cream and butter with hazelnuts and chestnuts.

FOR THE HAZELNUT CREAM (makes 5½oz/150g):
⅓ cup (50g) roasted, skinned hazelnuts
6 tbsp (100g) light cream

FOR THE DOUGH:
1¾ cups (250g) bread flour (61%)
⅔ cup (80g) whole-wheat bread flour (20%)
3oz (75g) chestnut flour (19%)
1 tsp fine sea salt (2%)
¾ cup (175g) water at 68°F (44%)
1½ tsp fresh yeast, crumbled (2%)
5½oz (150g) hazelnut cream (37%)
4oz (120g) white leaven (30%) (see pages 25–27)
1¼ tbsp unsalted butter, melted (5%)
1 cup (150g) cooked chestnuts, crumbled into pieces (37%)

FOR THE HAZELNUT CREAM Make a paste with the hazelnuts and cream, either in a mortar and pestle or quickly in a blender.

FOR THE DOUGH In a large bowl, combine the flours and salt. In another bowl, beat the water, yeast, hazelnut cream, and leaven, then tip this into the dry ingredients. Mix this well with your hands until you have a soft, sticky dough, then scrape any dough from your fingers into the bowl, cover and leave for 10 minutes.

Tip the cooled, melted butter over the top of the dough and, working with your fingers, mix it in evenly. Rub 1 tsp of corn or olive oil on the work-surface and knead the dough on the oiled surface for 10 seconds, ending with the dough in a smooth, round ball. Clean and dry the bowl, then rub lightly with a tsp of oil. Leave the dough in the bowl for an additional 10 minutes. Knead the dough again on the oiled surface, returning the shape to a smooth, round ball. Leave in the bowl, covered, for 30 minutes in a warm (70–77°F) place.

Place the dough back on the lightly oiled surface. With your fingers, press the dough out into a rough 8 x 12in rectangle. Sprinkle the chestnut pieces over the surface of the dough, then roll the dough up tightly so that the chestnuts are trapped inside. Fold the dough roll up by thirds, then tap the dough down to seal the nuts inside. Return the dough to the bowl, cover it with a cloth, and leave for 30 minutes.

Divide the dough into two equal pieces. Shape each into a baton (see page 21). Cover and leave each loaf to rise, seam-side-up, in a basket or tucked in a flour-rubbed cloth for 45 minutes.

Preheat the oven to 410°F. Upturn the loaves onto a baking sheet and slash the top with a sharp blade. Lightly spray the surface of each loaf with a mist of water and bake in the center of the oven for 20 minutes. Reduce the heat to 375°F and bake for an additional 45 minutes. The crust will darken considerably due to the butter and cream in the dough. Allow to cool on a wire rack.

Sweet black currant crown

All the ingredients for this loaf were found on Camilla Plum's farm, Fuglebjerggaard (see pages 70–72). The rye flour was freshly milled by her partner, Per Koelster, and the grains were soaked in his home-brewed ale; ripe fruit sagged each willowy branch of the scraggly black currant bushes; there was sweet butter, and the fresh eggs I collected from hens that pecked around the apple orchard. It is a large, beautiful loaf filled with good memories, and a loaf that makes good use of the fruit of late summer. Serve it warm.

TIP The loaf can be made as small or as large as you wish just by changing the number of jelly-filled balls you fill it with. It can be easily made in a loaf pan or a round spring-form cake pan. Just don't pack it too tightly, to allow the balls room to rise.

clarified butter to oil the pan
2lb (900g) sweet yeasted butter dough (100%) (see page 145)
6 tbsp black currant jelly (11%)
⅔ cup (100g) fresh black currants (11%)
½ cup (100g) soft brown sugar (11%)
3½oz (100g) beer-soaked rye grains, cooked until soft (11%) (see page 49)

Brush the inside of an 8in diameter *kugelhopf* mold with clarified butter. The loaf will produce a lot of rich syrup, which can cause the bread to stick to the pan, which oiling prevents.

Divide the dough into 18 pieces, each weighing 2oz (50g). Lightly flour the palm of your hand, and roll each piece of dough into a ball. Press your thumb into each ball to make a deep indent and put a scant tsp of black currant jelly into each one. Pinch the edges together so that the jelly is neatly sealed inside the ball of dough. Continue with all the pieces of dough until every one is filled and sealed.

Mix the black currants, brown sugar, and soft rye grains. Place three balls of dough equally spaced apart in the bottom of the buttered mold, then sprinkle with a fifth of the sugar, grain and blackcurrant mix. Fill the spaces in-between with three more balls, pressing them lightly down and sprinkling them again with a fifth of the sugar, grain and blackcurrant mix. Repeat until you have packed all of the dough balls into the mold together with the sugar mix. Cover the container and leave in a warm place until the dough has almost doubled in height.

Preheat the oven to 400°F. Place the pan on a baking sheet and bake in the center of the oven for 25 minutes. Reduce the heat to 330°F and bake for an additional 25 minutes. Allow to settle for 2 minutes in the pan, then carefully upturn the bread onto a serving tray, easing it gently out of the mold and being careful to protect your hands from any hot syrup. Serve while hot or warm, with a little custard or cream.

Onion and bay loaf

Bay is a good flavor to partner with onions and milk. It has that soothing aroma that makes a good white sauce taste homely, and in this loaf it adds an unusual fragrance to the crumb. The loaf is perfect toasted to serve with a good smoked kipper, grilled field mushrooms, and melted butter.

FOR THE ONIONS: (makes 10oz/280g)

10oz (280g) white onions, diced into ¾in pieces

scant 1¼ cups (280g) whole milk

3 bay leaves

FOR THE DOUGH:

1 scant cup (100g) whole-wheat bread flour (20%)

3 cups (400g) bread flour (80%)

1½ tsp fine sea salt (1%)

1¼ tsp fresh yeast, crumbled (1%)

1 cup (250g) milk from the onions (50%)

5½oz (150g) white leaven (30%)
 (see pages 25–27)

10oz (280g) cooked onions (56%)

Place the chopped onions, milk, and bay leaves in a saucepan and bring to a boil, then remove from the heat and allow to cool for about 30 minutes. Pour through a strainer to separate the onions and bay leaves from the milk. Reserve the milk, for use in the dough.

In a large bowl, combine the flour and salt. In another bowl, beat the yeast with 1 cup (250g) of the milk in which the onions have been cooked. Beat in the leaven until the mixture is smooth, then finally add the onions and stir. Pour the wet ingredients in with the flour, and stir until you have a soft sticky dough. Scrape any dough from your fingers into the bowl, then cover and leave for 10 minutes.

Rub 1 tsp of corn or olive oil on the work-surface and knead the dough on the oiled surface for 10 seconds, ending with the dough in a smooth, round ball. Clean and dry the bowl, then rub with a tsp of oil. Return the dough to the bowl and leave for an additional 10 minutes. Remove the dough and knead once more on the oiled surface, returning the shape of the dough to a smooth, round ball. Place it back in the bowl, cover, and leave for 1 hour in a warm (70–77°F) place.

Line a deep 8in diameter bowl with a flour-rubbed dishtowel. Lightly flour the work-surface and shape the dough into a ball (see page 21). Place the ball of dough seam-side-upward into the cloth, then cover it with the exposed corners of the dishtowel. Leave the bowl in a warm (70–77°F) place for 1½ hours, or until the loaf has doubled in height.

Preheat the oven to 410°F. Upturn the loaf onto a semolina-dusted baking sheet. Spray the upper surface of the dough with a fine mist of water, then place the sheet in the center of the oven and bake for 20 minutes. Reduce the heat to 375°F and bake for an additional 30 minutes, until the loaf is a good dark brown color. Allow to cool on a wire rack.

Almond-milk loaf

2 cups (250g) all-purpose flour (50%)
1¾ cups (250g) bread flour (50%)
1½ tsp fine sea salt (2%)
1 cup (150g) skinned almonds (30%)

1½ tbsp superfine sugar (4%)
1⅓ cups (325g) water at 68°F (65%)
2 tsp fresh yeast, crumbled (2%)

Eliza Acton, in her *English Bread Book*, describes an almond bread recipe entitled "Turkish Bread." Though I can't find a mention of such a loaf in any books on Turkish cuisine, they may have existed: Victorian England had such a fascination with the architecture and stories of the Levant that the desire to attribute recipes to these places must have been alluring. This recipe takes a type of nut milk sold in Italy—a marzipan that is mixed with water to make a iced summertime drink—and uses it as the liquid to moisten the dough. Though it is not a sweet dough, the almonds increase the protein slightly and make it a good, filling loaf.

TIP For the bread in the photograph, I've used a Pullman pan. This is a bread-baking pan with a lid that slides over the top, which you can buy at specialty kitchenware stores or by mail order.

Mix the two flours with the salt in a large bowl. Using a mortar and pestle, or a blender, grind the almonds to a creamy paste with the sugar and 6 tbsp of the water, then beat in the remaining water and the yeast. Stir this liquid in with the dry ingredients and mix it all together until you have a soft, sticky dough. Scrape any dough from your fingers into the bowl, then cover and leave for 10 minutes.

Rub 1 tsp of corn or olive oil on the work-surface and knead the dough on the oiled surface for 10 seconds, ending with the dough in a smooth, round ball. Clean and dry the bowl, then rub lightly with a tsp of oil. Return the dough to the bowl and leave for an additional 10 minutes. Remove the dough, knead once more on the oiled surface, returning the shape of the dough to a smooth, round ball. Place it back in the bowl, cover, and leave for 1 hour in a warm (70–77°F) place.

Oil and flour a deep loaf pan (4 x 7in). Lightly flour the work-surface and shape the dough into a baton (see page 21). This time, however, tap the ends in before rolling it back and forth to form a smooth cylinder the same length as the pan. Drop the dough seam-side-upward into the pan, and allow to rise for 1½ hours or until doubled in height. If you're using a Pullman pan, add the greased lid at this point.

Preheat the oven to 410°F. For an open top loaf, lightly dust the dough surface with flour. For a closed Pullman loaf, just check that the dough nearly touches the lid. Bake in the center of the oven for 25 minutes, then reduce the heat to 375°F and bake for an additional 20 minutes, until the loaf is a good golden-brown. Allow to cool on a wire rack.

White potato stottie cake

The stottie cake is the flatbread from the city of heroes, Newcastle upon Tyne. Although almost unknown outside its home region, we should recognize it as one of the great breads of Europe. It is a thin disc of good white dough that is baked on hot stones in the oven before being flipped and baked on the other side. Ian Gregg's eponymous bakery used to have an oven in the old Grainger market, just up from the tripe stall, and here the bakers would flip stotties during the day. At its best, the stottie is like a large perfect white muffin (not the cake sort), tinged brown on both sides with a very soft tender crumb. As cooked potatoes would have been added to the dough on occasion, I've included them in this recipe to add heartiness to a simple loaf. Rather than attempting to flip these, I find it best to lay a second sheet on top of the unbaked stotties, weighted down by something heavy and ovenproof to hold it in place during baking.

3⅔ cups (500g) bread flour (100%)
1½ tsp fine sea salt (2%)
1¼ cups (300g) water at 68°F (60%)
1½ cups (300g) mashed cooked potato (60%)
2 tsp fresh yeast, crumbled (2%)

In a large bowl, mix the flour with the salt. In another bowl, beat the water with the mashed potato and yeast, then pour this in with the dry ingredients. Stir the mixture together with your hands until you have a soft, sticky dough.

Rub 1 tsp of corn or olive oil on the work-surface and knead the dough on the oiled surface for 10 seconds, ending with the dough in a smooth, round ball. Clean and dry the bowl, then rub lightly with a tsp of oil. Return the dough to the bowl and leave for an additional 10 minutes. Remove the dough, knead once more on the oiled surface, returning the shape of the dough to a smooth round ball. Place it back in the bowl, cover, and leave for 1 hour in a warm (70–77°F) place.

Divide the dough into four equal pieces, each roughly 10oz (280g) in weight. On a lightly floured surface roll each piece into a round disc measuring 6in in diameter. Lay each disc on a floured tray. Cover with a cloth and allow to rise for 45 minutes, or until almost doubled in height.

Preheat the oven to 410°F. Uncover the unbaked stotties and lightly sift flour evenly over the upper surface of each loaf. Place a clean baking sheet directly on top of the dough, so it is sandwiched between two sheets of metal, and bake in the center of the oven for 30 minutes. Carefully lift off the upper sheet and, using a spatula, transfer the baked stotties to a wire rack. When cool, wrap well to stop them from drying out.

Layered apple and custard loaf

Thick custard, brown sugar, and good dessert apples are layered between discs of buttery dough, then baked to form one loaf. This is perhaps not the most delicate of breads but, like rice pudding or plum *clafoutis*, it is good, hearty stodge—perfect after an energetic day in the field or garden; the sort of fruit-bread children seem to understand very well.

1lb (450g) sweet yeasted butter dough (see page 145)

1½lb (700g) pastry custard (see page 187)

5 good dessert apples

½ cup (100g) soft brown sugar

Line the base and sides of a 10in springform cake pan with non-stick parchment paper (or well buttered brown paper). Peel and core the apples and cut into slices.

Divide the dough into three pieces, each weighing roughly 5½oz (150g). On a flour-dusted work-surface roll each piece of dough out into a disc 10in in diameter (the same size as the cake pan). Place one in the bottom of the pan, then spread a third of the custard over the surface. Cover the custard with a third of the apples, then sprinkle with a third of the sugar. Repeat with the other pieces of dough, the remaining custard, apples, and sugar. Sprinkle the upper surface of the unbaked loaf with the last of the sugar, and leave in a warm (70–77°F) place to rise for 1½ hours.

Preheat the oven to 400°F. Bake on a rack in the center of the oven for 10 minutes. Reduce the heat to 330°F and bake for an additional 35 minutes, covering the top of the cake at the end if it gets too brown. Leave in the pan to cool, and serve when warm.

Herbs, spices, & fragrances

In Yaroslava Kharuk's kitchen in the Ukrainian city of Ivano-Frankivsk, the garden herbs were spread out over trays lined with white cloth and left to dry slowly in the warmth. It was the end of fall. The trees outside were stripped bare by the wind and the soil had already begun to harden in the cold. But here in the heat of kitchen, the last remaining edible leaves were being stored to ensure that some of that flavor could be added to winter foods.

For flavoring, we take the bright-tasting ingredients of one season and apply them to another less palatable food, modifying and tempering the flavor so that it has the hint of something familiar and appealing. Spices and herbs, when combined with a dominant helping of sugar or salt, nudge foods toward either sweet or savory: sweet cinnamon and apple, for example, or savory mustard and apple.

What these additional flavors and aromas do is offer us a choice, multiplying the possible dishes that can be created from a small garden and extending the number of breads that can be baked from a single grain. Sometimes herbs and spices add a playful novelty to a loaf's taste, or establish its tradition, or act solely as a marker to advise a customer or assistant in a bakery what type of loaf it is.

There are great dishes and breads that combine many spices, for example the Bavarian breads that use a complex mixture of fennel, caraway, anise, and dill, and the many different spice mixtures for gingerbread. But don't overlook the value of a herb, spice, vegetable, or strongly scented oil. Coriander alone can make a notable rye bread by imparting a fragrant bitter taste, a little like the white pith of an orange, to a dark loaf.

Black pepper pancakes

Thin, crisp-edged pancakes or crêpes are, like a loaf at the table, an elegant way of extending more expensive ingredients. Wrapped around spinach and ricotta, or braised endive and bacon, they turn the fillings into simple, pleasurable meals.

2 medium eggs (96%)
1¼ cups (300g) milk at 68°F (240%)
1 cup (125g) all-purpose flour (100%)
½ tsp fine sea salt (2%)
¾ tsp freshly ground black pepper (3%)
2 tbsp unsalted butter, melted (20%)

In a bowl or pitcher, beat the eggs with the milk. Sift the flour and beat this into the liquid. Stir in the salt and black pepper, then beat in the melted butter. Cover the bowl and refrigerate for 2 hours.

Preheat a non-stick skillet, and add 1 tsp of olive oil, lard, or butter, heating until it is almost smoking hot. Remove the pan from the heat and rub any excess oil from the surface using a few sheets of scrunched-up kitchen towel.

Ladle 2–3 tbsp batter into the center of the pan, turning it so the batter spreads thinly. Return to the heat and cook for 2–3 minutes, until the edges are crisp and brown and the surface is broken with air bubbles that go through to the base of the pan. With a spatula, loosen the pancake from the skillet and flip over. Cook for another minute, or until both sides are brown. Sometimes the first pancake sticks a little, but if it does simply rub off any stuck bits and rub oil once more onto the surface.

Remove the pancake from the pan, place on a plate, and cover with a cloth while you cook the remaining pancakes.

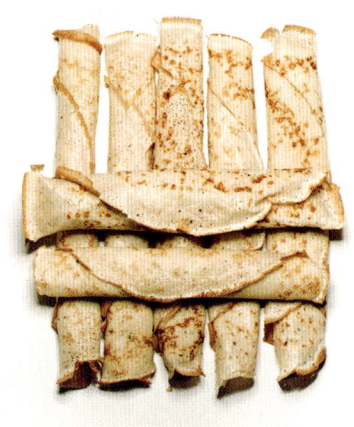

Sweet saffron bread

This bread uses what bakers call a "sponge": equal quantities of flour and liquid mixed with a small amount of yeast. If you look at the procedure to make a naturally leavened bread (see page 28), this is similar but mightily accelerated.

FOR THE SPONGE:
6 tbsp (100g) milk at 68°F
¾ tsp fresh yeast, crumbled
¾ cup (100g) all-purpose flour

FOR THE DOUGH:
12 threads saffron (0.5%)
¼ tbsp boiling water (24%)
1¾ cups (250g) bread flour (100%)
2 tbsp superfine sugar (10%)
scant ½ tsp fine sea salt (1%)
1 tbsp unsalted butter, softened (12%)
⅔ cup (150g) milk at 68°F (60%)
  the sponge (80%)
⅔ cup (100g) currants (40%)
cornmeal for dusting the baking sheet
egg wash for glazing (see page 187)

FOR THE SPONGE In a bowl, beat together the milk, yeast, and flour until smooth. Cover and leave in a warm (77°F) place for 1 hour, until the mixture is bubbling and smells yeasty.

FOR THE DOUGH Cover the saffron with the boiling water and leave for 10 minutes to infuse.

In a large bowl, combine the flour with the sugar and salt. Break the butter into small pieces, then rub this through the flour until it disappears and no lumps remain. In another bowl or pitcher, beat the milk with the saffron water, then stir this in with the sponge. Keep stirring until the mixture has evenly combined, then mix in the currants. Pour this liquid in with the flour and stir until you have a soft, sticky dough. Scrape any dough from your fingers into the bowl, cover and leave for 10 minutes.

Rub 1 tsp of corn or olive oil on the work-surface and knead the dough on the oiled surface for 10 seconds, ending with it in a smooth, round ball. Clean and dry the bowl, then rub lightly with a tsp of oil. Return the dough to the bowl and leave for an additional 10 minutes. Remove the dough and knead once more on the oiled surface, returning the shape of the dough to a smooth round ball. Place it back in the bowl, cover, and leave for 1 hour in a warm (70–77°F) place.

Lightly dust the work-surface and shape the dough into a baton (see page 21). Cover with a cloth and leave for 10 minutes for the dough to soften and relax. Roll the dough out using your floured hands until you have a piece measuring 20in long. Spiral each end, in opposite directions, until you have an elaborate "S" shape. Sprinkle a large 12 x 16in baking sheet with cornmeal, then place the dough in the center of the tray. Cover lightly with a cloth and leave for 1 hour, or until almost doubled in height.

Preheat the oven to 410°F. Uncover the loaf and brush the surface gently and lightly with egg wash. Bake in the center of the oven for 30 minutes, then reduce the heat to 375°F and bake for an additional 15–20 minutes, until the loaf is a good brown color, feels light in weight, and sounds hollow when tapped on the base. Allow to cool on a wire rack.

Parsley potato cakes

This is a potato scone, fried in a dry pan over a gentle heat. If you're feeling nimble you could bake it, as it would have traditionally been, on a griddle or girdle. But the handle on the skillet makes it easier to flip. Non-stick pans make this task easy, but if you don't have one then use a heavy iron skillet that has been oiled and heated to a high temperature, then allowed to cool before using. This makes food less likely to stick. Serve like "bubble and squeak" for a late big breakfast, together with bacon, eggs, and broiled large field mushrooms.

1 cup (125g) all-purpose flour (100%)
½ tsp baking soda (2%)
½ tsp fine sea salt (2%)
¼ cup (60g) unsalted butter, softened (48%)
1¼ cups (250g) mashed cooked potato (200%)
1 medium egg (48%)
6 tbsp (100g) milk at 68°F (80%)
2 tbsp fresh chopped parsley (4%)
dripping or oil

In a large bowl, combine the flour with the soda and salt. Break the butter into small pieces and rub it into the flour mixture until no lumps remain. In another bowl, beat the mashed potato with the egg, then beat in the milk and parsley. Pour this in with the dry ingredients and stir until you have an evenly combined, soft and sticky dough.

Take a large skillet, ideally one with a close-fitting lid. Melt 1 tbsp of dripping (or sunflower oil) in the pan, then swirl the pan to coat the base evenly. Place this over a heat-diffusing plate on a low heat, and scrape the dough into the pan. Quickly pat the surface smooth with a spatula, then allow to cook over a gentle heat for 4–5 minutes, preferably with a lid on. As you need to cook the flour out, it is vital to keep the heat low and extend the cooking time. Aim for a crisp, slightly brown base to the cake after about 5 minutes.

Liberally oil a large dinner plate. Place this over the top of the skillet then, using a thick cloth, flip the pan over so that the cake falls down onto the plate. Slide the upturned cake back into the pan, return to the heat, and cook for an additional 4–5 minutes.

To serve, flip the cake out onto the oiled plate and cut into wedges, or simply put crisp bacon, broiled mushrooms, and tomatoes on the top and serve it straight out of the pan—but that might be too piggy!

Chelsea buns

The traditional Chelsea bun has a slight lemon flavor, and the dough would be dusted with nutmeg before rolling. By the early 20th century, cinnamon became the preferred spice. I've used nutmeg, as I prefer its taste combined with lemon in the bun. Lard would have been used for rolling, but I prefer butter, or at least half butter and half lard.

FOR THE FILLING:

¼ cup (50g) soft brown sugar

¼ cup (50g) superfine sugar

¼ cup (50g) unsalted butter, softened

zest of ¼ lemon

¼ tsp freshly grated nutmeg

⅔ cup (100g) currants

TO SERVE:

melted butter for greasing the pan

superfine sugar for dredging

FOR THE DOUGH:

1¼ cups (150g) all-purpose flour (33%)

2 cups (300g) bread flour (67%)

1 tsp fine sea salt (2%)

5 tbsp (75g) milk at 68°F (16%)

5 tbsp (75g) water at 68°F (16%)

2 medium eggs (27%)

2½ tbsp corn syrup (11%)

2 tsp fresh yeast, crumbled (3%)

FOR THE FILLING Combine all the ingredients apart from the currants until you have a soft paste. Leave this in a warm (70–77°F) place while you make the dough.

FOR THE DOUGH In a large bowl, combine the two flours with the salt. In another bowl or pitcher, place the milk, water, eggs, corn syrup, and fresh yeast. Beat until smooth. Pour the liquid in with the dry ingredients and stir with your hands until you have a soft, sticky dough. Scrape any dough from your fingers into the bowl, cover and leave for 10 minutes.

Rub 1 tsp of corn or olive oil on the work-surface and knead the dough on the oiled surface for 10 seconds, ending with the dough in a smooth, round ball. Clean and dry the bowl, then rub lightly with a tsp of oil. Return the dough to the bowl and leave for an additional 10 minutes. Knead the dough once more on the oiled surface, returning it to a smooth, round ball. Place it back in the bowl, cover, and leave for 1 hour in a warm (70–77°F) place.

Line a 12in square cake pan with non-stick parchment paper on the base and brush the paper and sides with melted butter. Lightly dust the work-surface with flour and roll the dough out into a 14in square. Crumble the filling over the dough and press it down into the surface, then scatter the currants evenly across the dough. Roll the dough up tightly from one end. Cut the dough into nine equal pieces, then place these (three across by three down) in the pan. Cover the pan with a cloth and allow to rise for 1 hour.

Preheat the oven to 410°F. Uncover the pan and dredge the surface of the dough with superfine sugar. Bake in the center of the oven for 30 minutes, then reduce the heat to 375°F and bake for an additional 15–20 minutes, until the buns are a good brown color on top. Allow to cool on a wire rack for 10 minutes. Brush the top of the buns with sugar glaze (see page 188) and serve warm.

Rye with coriander

FOR THE SPONGE:

5½oz (150g) rye leaven
   (see pages 25–27 and 31)
2 scant cups (450g) water at 68°F
½ tsp fresh yeast, crumbled
1½ tbsp bran
2oz (50g) ground malted barley or rye
   (see page 38–39)

FOR THE DOUGH:

2 tsp coriander seeds (2%)
2 cups (250g) light rye flour (62.5%)
1 cup (150g) bread flour (37.5%)
1 tsp fine sea salt (2%)
the sponge (165%)

This dark bread is reminiscent of the bread served in small, traditional cafeterias in Russia and the Ukraine, and it is an acquired taste. It has a hefty dose of freshly ground coriander seed worked into the dough, giving the crumb a slight bitterness, like the white pith of an orange. It offsets the sweetness of malt and is a traditional flavoring for some old ales and beers.

FOR THE SPONGE In a bowl, beat together the rye leaven, water, yeast, bran, and malt until you have a smooth paste. Cover and leave for 1½ hours, or until bubbly and fermenting.

FOR THE DOUGH In a large bowl, combine the coriander seeds, rye and bread flours, and salt. Toss with your fingers until lightly combined, then mix in the sponge liquid, squeezing the mixture through your fingertips until evenly combined. Scrape any dough from your fingers into the bowl, cover and leave for 10 minutes.

Rub 1 tsp of corn or olive oil on the work-surface and knead the dough on the oiled surface for 10 seconds, ending with a smooth, round ball. Clean and dry the bowl, then rub lightly with a tsp of oil. Return the dough to the bowl, cover and leave for an additional 10 minutes. Remove the dough and knead once more on the oiled surface, returning the shape of the dough to a smooth, round ball. Place it back in the bowl, cover, and leave for 1 hour in a warm (70–77°F) place.

Oil and flour an 8 x 4in oblong loaf pan. Lightly dust the work-surface with flour and shape the dough into a baton (see page 21). Drop the baton into the pan, and press it down with your knuckles until it sits evenly inside. Cover the pan lightly with a cloth and leave in a warm (70–77°F) place for ¾ hour, or until risen by a third and just about over the top of the pan.

Preheat the oven to 410°F. Uncover the loaf and, using a sharp blade, slash down the middle of the top of the loaf. Mist the upper surface of the dough lightly with water. Bake in the center of the oven for 30 minutes, then reduce the heat to 375°F and bake for an additional 15–20 minutes, until the loaf is a good brown color, feels light in weight, and sounds hollow when tapped on the base. Allow to cool on a wire rack for 10 minutes, then remove the loaf from the pan and leave it to cool upright on a wire rack.

Orange and almond cake

This is a dessert bread. The sweet little cakes are served with cream and fruit, or cut into wedges and spread with unsalted butter and lemon curd. Or you could use the dough as a soft top over a dish of poached apricots, baking them both until the crust is crisp and golden and the apricots bubbling hot.

TIP As an alternative to making four round cakes, you can simply pat the dough out onto a paper-lined baking sheet in one piece, dredge it with sugar and bake, then cut into squares or fingers while still warm.

⅔ cup (100g) blanched and peeled almonds, ground (66%)
1¼ cups (150g) all-purpose flour (100%)
⅓ cup (80g) superfine sugar (53%)
1 tsp baking powder (2%)
¼ cup (50g) unsalted butter, softened (33%)
3 tbsp (50g) heavy cream (33%)
4 tbsp (60g) whole milk at 68°F (40%)
zest of 1 orange (2%)
slivered almonds
superfine sugar for dredging

Preheat the oven to 425°F. Line a 16 x 12in baking sheet with non-stick parchment paper.

In a large bowl, combine the ground almonds, flour, sugar, and baking powder. Toss with your fingers until evenly combined, then break the butter into small pieces and rub this through the flour until the mixture resembles fine bread crumbs.

In a pitcher or another bowl, beat the cream with the milk and orange zest. Stir this in with the dry ingredients until you have a soft smooth paste.

Scrape the dough out onto a plate and divide into four even pieces. Wet your fingers and shape each piece into a ball, then squash it flat on the paper-lined sheet so that it sits ¾in high by about 3in in diameter. Strew a few slivers of almond on top of each cake, and dredge heavily with the additional superfine sugar.

Bake in the center of the oven for 18–20 minutes, or until risen and golden brown on top. Remove from the oven and, after a few moments, transfer the cakes to a wire cooling rack. When warm, serve with a little softly whipped cream and soft fruit.

Lemon barley cob

This is a hearty loaf, though its name might suggest a delicate appearance. It is sprinkled with coarse flakes of sea salt before baking, which stick out like prickles on the tan-brown crust. Barley benefits from a little acidity and the grated zest of lemon, plus the juice in the dough, picks the flavor up and lends it a gentle rye-like tang. Serve this as a sandwich bread, filled with oily, bright things such as grilled peppers and soft olive paste, together with cheese and ham. A handful of soft lamb's lettuce between the slices is the best finish.

1 scant cup (100g) barley flour (40%)
1 cup (150g) bread flour (60%)
¾ tsp fine sea salt (2%)
5½oz (150g) white leaven (60%) (see pages 25–27)
⅔ cup (150g) water at 68°F (60%)
1 tbsp lemon juice (6%)
zest of 1 lemon (2%)
1½ tbsp honey (12%)
¾ tsp fresh yeast, crumbled (1%)
coarse sea salt for sprinkling

In a large bowl, combine the barley and bread flours with the salt. In another bowl or pitcher, beat together the leaven, water, lemon juice and zest, honey, and yeast until smooth and combined. Stir this liquid in with the dry ingredients and mix until you have an evenly-combined, soft and sticky dough. Scrape any dough from your fingers into the bowl, cover and leave for 10 minutes.

Rub 1 tsp of corn or olive oil on the work-surface and knead the dough on the oiled surface for 10 seconds, ending with a smooth, round ball. Clean and dry the bowl, then rub lightly with a tsp of oil. Return the dough to the bowl and leave for an additional 10 minutes. Knead the dough once more on the oiled surface, returning the shape of the dough to a smooth, round ball. Place it back in the bowl, cover and leave for 1 hour in a warm (70–77°F) place.

Lightly dust the work-surface and shape the dough into a baton (see page 21). Rub flour into a dishtowel (or use a linen-lined rising basket) and place the dough inside, seam-side-up. Wrap the dough up snugly in the cloth, and allow to rise for 1½ hours, or until almost doubled in height.

Preheat the oven to 410°F. Upturn the loaf onto a flour- or semolina-dusted baking sheet, spray (or brush) the upper surface with water, then sprinkle the surface with flaked crystal sea salt. Using a sharp blade, slash the loaf along the length. Bake in the center of the oven for 30 minutes, then reduce the heat to 375°F and bake for an additional 15–20 minutes, until the loaf is a good brown color, feels light in weight, and sounds hollow when tapped on the base. Allow to cool on a wire rack.

White thyme bread

Jack Lang, a passionate home baker in Cambridge, has a wood-fired oven in his garden, sitting under the apple trees like an old, miniature house, with a pointed roof covered in different varieties of thyme. In summer, small flowers appear dotted among the leaves, their roots tickled by the insulated warmth of the oven dome below. Thyme is an excellent herb to mix into an olive oil dough as the oil helps spread the flavor from the herb through every slice. For this bread I use picholine olives, which have a crisp, rather than soft, texture, and a sweet, nutty taste. Pit these by hand, pressing them firmly down onto the work-surface to split them in two, then picking out the pit with your fingers. Tricky, I know, but the flavor is worth the effort.

2½ cups (350g) bread flour (100%)
1 tsp fine sea salt (2%)
⅔ cup (150g) water at 68°F (43%)
5¼oz (150g) white leaven (43%)
  (see pages 25–27)
½ tsp fresh yeast, crumbled (1%)
1½ tbsp (25g) extra virgin olive oil (7%)
⅔ cup (100g) pitted green olives (29%)
1 tsp chopped fresh thyme (1.5%)
cornmeal for dusting

In a large bowl, combine the flour with the salt, tossing it together with your fingers. In another bowl, beat together the water, leaven, yeast, olive oil, the olives, and thyme. Pour this liquid in with the flour, then stir with your hands until you have a soft, sticky dough. Scrape any dough from your fingers into the bowl, cover and leave for 10 minutes.

Rub a good tsp of olive oil onto a clean work-surface and lightly knead the dough on the oiled surface for 10 seconds. Return the dough to the bowl and leave for 10 minutes. Repeat this brief kneading, using a little more oil if necessary, then return the dough to the bowl and leave for an additional 10 minutes. Knead the dough once more on the oiled surface, return to the bowl and leave for another 10 minutes.

Generously oil a lipped tray. Place the dough seam-side-down on the oiled tray and pat it out into a rectangle, then fold it in by thirds each way. Flip the dough over so that the seam side faces down. Place the cloth back over the dough and leave for 1 hour in a warm (70–77°F) place. Stretch the dough, fold as before, and leave again for an hour. Repeat this stretching and folding once more and allow to rise again for an hour. Each time you gently stretch and fold the dough, try to keep as much air in it as you can and avoid flattening it. It is important that the temperature of the dough does not rise above 70–77°F; it should always feel cool to the touch. When the dough is ready, a cut into the center should reveal a network of holes.

Lightly oil a 12 x 8in baking sheet, and sprinkle the surface lightly with cornmeal. Flip the dough out onto the center of the sheet, then dimple the surface with your fingertips to slightly flatten it. Sprinkle the upper surface of the dough with cornmeal too, then loosely cover the dough with a cloth and leave for 30–45 minutes, ideally in a warmer place near the oven at 77–82°F.

Preheat the oven to 425°F. Uncover the dough and bake in the center of the oven for 40 minutes, or until the upper surface is a good golden brown. Using a spatula, ease the bread from the sheet and allow it to cool on a wire rack.

Sweden

There is an impressive, modern artisan baking culture in Sweden, and much of it stems from the work and influence of one man: Jan Hedh. Hedh is an accomplished craftsman and his bakery, near the coastal town of Ystad, has produced many of the region's talented bakers. His approach to bread-making—to respect the provenance of ingredients and to maintain traditional Swedish recipes and techniques—has earned him the deep respect, in turn, of the "new guard" bakers in Stockholm. He is a gentle giant of a man, deeply knowledgeable and experienced, and we drank mightily into the night as we talked about rye breads, baking, and life.

Early the following morning, we make our way to Hedh's bakery, Olof Viktors, in Glemmingebro. Standing beside a patch of woodland is a traditional large, square, white-brick building with gates on one side leading to a courtyard in the center. At one end stands the bakery, with a modern wood-fired oven, designed by Hedh, which is fueled by timber from the forest. His young team had started early this morning. The day before, he had baked a dozen saffron loaves, curled and twisted and egg glazed before baking. They look like bronze artefacts, somewhat medieval and regal.

By the door, hanging on a wooden rod, are discs of *knäckebröd*, Swedish rye crisp bread that dry as they hang in the warm air. Crisp breads traditionally kept the harvested grain edible through the winter months and were hung up to keep them away from vermin. Though now we think of crisp breads as little oblongs wrapped in paper, with the bite and crunch of potato chips, they were once far sturdier—and they still are today, when made by small artisan bakers in Sweden.

Swedish food writer Dag Hermelin suggested I go to visit Roslagsbröd, where the best *knäckebröd* in Sweden is made. The bakery is in a town called Gimo, north of Stockholm, and I reckoned on a few hours traveling time. The trip involved a train, then a bus, then a car—a combination that seemed sure to swallow the hours. But here technology lives up to its promise and all the connections, and the time taken to make them (even footsteps along the snow-covered bus depot), are measured and accounted for. The winter sun stays low during the day and skates across the horizon on a pink-hued path; the trip seemed to hover in a twilight moment, like those ever-lasting sunsets you view from the window of a jet plane.

LEFT, FROM TOP: Johan Sörbergs; Leif Torstensson; Jonas Adolffson; Dag Hermelin; Jan Hedh. ABOVE, FROM TOP: *knäckebröd*; Johan Sörbergs breaking crisp bread; Sörbergs' rye flatbreads; salty sweet rye; OPPOSITE, CLOCKWISE FROM TOP LEFT: Chef Östen Brolin and baker Richard Bingham at Vete Katten in Stockholm; *knäckebröd* at Roslagsbröd; the window at Riddarbageriet; spiced rye flatbread; Jan Hedh's wheaten loaf; soft anise and fennel *oälkaka*; saffron crown; sweet saffron pastry; soft rye bread; apple Danish; *knäckebröd* at Hedh's bakery; baker at Riddarbageriet; sky in Gimo; caraway crisp bread at Riddarbageriet; CENTER: Johan Sörbergs and bakers at Riddarbageriet; Christmas wheat *knäckebröd* at Roslagsbröd.

The bakery stands in a small warehouse, which was built in 1922 by B. E. Sandstrom and his family and then renovated in 1996 after it was brought by Robert Saberski, who also reinstated the former baker, Leif Torstensson.

The bakery is mechanized, but only in the sense that a farmer with a plow is mechanized. Most of the machinery and the large oven date from its opening in the 1920s. A pinkish daylight streams in through large frosted windows around two sides; the walls are lined with glazed white oblong tiles coated with a dusting of rye flour.

The large, free-spinning bowl of a slow dough-mixer judders around as its curved wishbone blade flips the dough over and over. This mixture of rye, leaven, salt, and water is sloppy, like thick, green-gray porridge, and is scooped with a spade by baker Tobbe Engberg into a strange, aging Heath Robinson contraption (minus the buzzers and whistles) painted buttercup yellow. There, knobbly rollers run back and forth over the dough as it is scraped over a cloth belt. A continual dredging of coarse rye flour rains down to contain the stickiness, and a wheel rolls a round stamp across to make the distinctive gramophone record shape with a hole in the middle.

And there, at the end, with a flat shovel, is Leif, who scoops the flatbreads onto a dozen thin, wooden planks that sit 4in above each other on a trolley. These are wheeled into a warm, damp room, where they puff up from $\frac{1}{10}$in thick to double that. Then Leif scoops them deftly onto the wire grid of the oven and they travel through to be almost grilled in the intense heat. As the rye lacks the sugars that color wheaten breads, it takes a fierce heat to tinge the crust brown. They sit above the oven, in a practice dating back centuries, to crisp and dry.

Johan Sörbergs, a former student of Jan Hedh's, has set up a small bakery in the center of Stockholm that is unabashedly young, feisty, loud, and innovative—qualities rarely found in bakeries within traditional communities. At Riddarbageriet, even the windows that expose the workings to the street have a brazen appearance. Yet the chunks of sweet gingerbread, the paper-thin *knäckebröd* topped with local seeds and berries, and the little saffron buns curled into a snake-like "S" shape, all resolutely stem from heartfelt respect for Swedish culture. Johan is simply the provocateur that pushes it forward.

Johan and I talk about burnt-top breads, the now almost forbidden practice. Today burnt crusts are viewed as deadly at worst, and certainly a waste. But without the penetrating effect of the browning or charring, the crumb flavor is thin and wanting. "It is always a battle," says Johan. "I would prefer to bake darker, like all bakers, but we struggle with the customer's ever-heightened anxiety. Has there ever been a 'burnt bread' related illness?"

By 8am a queue of a dozen customers is standing out into the street, even though the temperature dips well below zero. Inside the few tables are filled with people chatting and feasting on sweet freshly-baked morning breads and hot coffee. This is modern baking, a re-establishment of the relationship between the customer and the craftsperson based on respect and trust. "Customers come in and ask me what to buy, what's good today," says Johan, "and I think it's because they believe that I'll tell them the truth. And you know what? I would be honest every time."

"Today burnt crusts are viewed as deadly at worst… But without the penetrating effect of the browning and charring, the crumb flavor is thin."

Mustard and corn rolls

These are perfect spread with butter and wedged with a slice of good fatty ham and small sprigs of crisp watercress.

FOR THE DOUGH:

1½ cups (200g) bread flour (80%)

¼ cup (50g) fine corn flour (20%)

¾ tsp fine sea salt (2%)

1 tsp English mustard powder (2%)

3½oz (100g) white leaven (40%)
  (see pages 25–7)

½ cup (125g) water at 68°F (50%)

¾ tsp fresh yeast, crumbled (1%)

FOR THE MUSTARD WASH:

1 tsp English mustard powder

2 tsp water

1 tbsp olive oil

In a large bowl, combine the bread and corn flours with the salt and mustard powder. In another bowl or pitcher, beat the leaven with the water and yeast. Pour the liquid in with the dry ingredients and stir well until you have a soft, sticky dough. Scrape any dough from your fingers into the bowl, cover, and leave for 10 minutes.

Rub 1 tsp of corn or olive oil on the work-surface and knead the dough on the oiled surface for 10 seconds, ending with a smooth, round ball. Clean and dry the bowl, then rub lightly with 1 tsp of oil. Return the dough to the bowl and leave for an additional 10 minutes. Remove the dough and knead on the oiled surface for 10 seconds, returning the shape of the dough to a smooth, round ball. Place it back in the bowl, cover, and leave for 1 hour in a warm (70–77°F) place.

Divide the dough into eight pieces, each weighing approximately 2oz (60g). Round each piece tightly into a ball, and then sit it on a lightly floured work-surface, covered with a cloth. Allow to rise for 45 minutes.

Mix together the ingredients for the mustard wash in a small ramekin.

Preheat the oven to 410°F. Lightly dust a 16 x 12in sheet with corn flour. With the handle of a wooden spoon, press down into each ball of dough until there is only a membrane left between the two halves, then brush along the indent with a little of the mustard wash. Press the two halves back together, then place the roll on the sheet. Repeat with the remaining dough balls.

Spray a fine mist of water on top of the unbaked rolls. Bake for 20 minutes, then reduce the heat to 375°F and bake for an additional 15–20 minutes, until the rolls are a good golden brown. Transfer the rolls onto a wire rack to cool.

Honey and ginger wafers

Gingerbread-making has almost become a lost art. There were once associations of gingerbread-makers, who perfected this quite separate skill. One book I have lists 30 different spice mixtures, suggesting that each baker saw the combination of imported spices as his signature. These little wafers are often decorated with something more complicated than the mark of a fork that I've made here. But there is something appealing—almost Celtic—about this cross pattern, and I like it. Store the gingerbread in an airtight box for a few days with half an apple to keep them soft and moist.

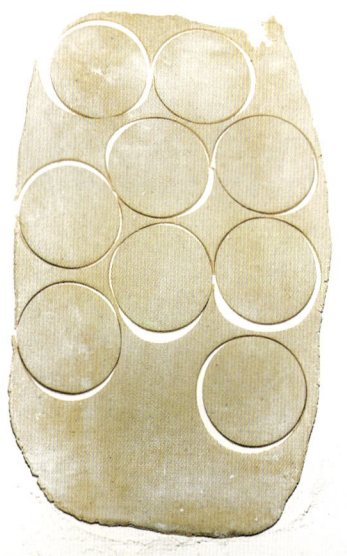

FOR THE SPICE MIX:
1 tsp whole coriander seeds
1 tsp ground cinnamon
¼ tsp grated nutmeg
¼ tsp whole black peppercorns
1 tsp ground ginger
2 cardamom pods
¼ tsp fennel seeds

FOR THE DOUGH:
⅔ cup (250g) honey (83%)
⅔ cup (150g) unsalted butter (50%)
2 tbsp heavy cream (10%)
1¼ cups (150g) all-purpose flour (50%)
1¼ cups (150g) light rye flour (50%)
1 tsp baking soda (1.5%)
½ cup (100g) soft brown sugar (33%)
spice mix (1.5%)

FOR THE GLAZE:
1 medium egg plus 1 egg yolk
1 tbsp water
¼ tsp fine sea salt

FOR THE SPICE MIX Pound the spice ingredients together in a mortar and pestle (or an electric spice grinder) until fine.

FOR THE DOUGH In a saucepan, heat the honey with the butter over a low heat until the butter has melted. Stir and leave to cool until warm, then stir in the heavy cream.

In a large bowl, combine the all-purpose and rye flours with the soda and soft brown sugar. Add the spice mix and toss with your fingers. Pour the warm honey, butter, and cream mixture in with the dry ingredients and stir until you have a smooth dough. Cover with a damp cloth, and allow it to sit for 20 minutes for the dough to soften, or wrap well and leave at room temperature (70°F) overnight.

Preheat the oven to 410°F. Lightly dust the work-surface with flour and place the dough on top of it. Using a rolling pin, roll out the dough to a thickness of ¼in. Using a 3in round cutter, cut rounds of dough and place them on a 12 x 16in sheet lined with non-stick parchment paper. You will need to bake these wafers in batches.

FOR THE GLAZE Beat the egg, yolk, water, and salt together, then brush the surface of each gingerbread with this egg wash. Use the prongs of a fork to make a cross mark in the surface of each wafer.

Bake in the center of the oven for 15 minutes, or until the egg wash on the surface is golden brown. Remove from the oven, leave the sheet for a minute for the wafers to firm, then using a spatula, transfer to a wire rack. Bake the remaining wafers in the same way and, when done and cool, pack them in an airtight container.

Garlic dumplings

1 cup (150g) bread flour (100%)
½ tsp fine sea salt (2%)
6 tbsp (100g) water at 68°F (67%)
¼ tsp fresh yeast, crumbled (2%)
1 clove garlic, crushed to a paste (3%)

In a bowl, combine the flour and salt, tossing them together with your fingers. In another bowl, beat together the water and yeast. Stir this liquid in with the flour until you have a soft, sticky dough. Wipe the crushed garlic over the surface of the dough, and work this in roughly. Scrape any dough from your fingers, cover the bowl and leave for 10 minutes.

Rub 1 tsp of corn or olive oil on the work-surface and knead the dough on the oiled surface for 10 seconds, ending with a smooth, round ball. Clean and dry the bowl, then rub lightly with a tsp of oil. Return the dough to the bowl and leave for an additional 10 minutes. Remove the dough, knead once more on the oiled surface, returning the shape of the dough to a smooth, round ball. Place it back in the bowl, cover, and leave for 1 hour in a warm (70–77°F) place.

Divide the dough into 12 or so pieces. The weight is not that important, but try to keep them all the same size so that they cook evenly. Lightly oil your hands and roll each piece into a smooth, tight ball. Place these on an oiled tray and cover with a cloth.

Set up your steamer (I use a stack of bamboo ones) or get your braise or broth simmering. Place the dumplings on an oiled plate in the steamer, or drop them into the braise or broth, and cook for 5 minutes, or until the dumplings have puffed up and slightly firmed. To check if they're done, take one out and cut it through with a sharp knife: it should have an open texture and a firm, very moist crumb. Serve immediately, or remove and cool, then heat to boiling when you're ready to serve.

A dumpling is a soft bread, either cooked with or alongside the meal, for example dropped into a thick simmering braise or stew. I have cooked these separately in a small steamer. This way they keep their shape, and look more dignified when plonked on the plate. Good winter fare.

TIP You can substitute half buttermilk (or milk) and half water for the water in the dough to make a richer dumpling.

The fat of the land

The flavor of a good fat gets even better when it is mixed with the taste of a grain. Equally, a starchy food is improved by the addition of some fat. A flour-thickened sauce gains a richness from butter, just as bacon fat lifts the peppery taste of lentils. But fat can taste excessive without starch, and perhaps it is not the loaf that likes the olive oil, but the oil that likes the loaf. I can eat and enjoy the grain on its own, but the fat often needs something to make it a pleasure.

Starches seem to round out the flavors of meat and fat, just as butter or oil can add a hint of good times to a plain loaf. When we describe this fatted taste as "rounded," what does that mean? Complete, balanced, whole, or simply finished, like the food from childhood, gilded to overcome a fear of plainness? As with hot buttered toast, we mean that the dish becomes good food when the fat is added; finally, and only then, is it ready to be eaten.

Oil worked into dough makes the taste comforting, and we feel wealthy; we add oil because we can afford to; because we have enough to share. We value the fat of the land and include it in breads that are eaten for significant events in our community, whether it is breads for the springtime, before Lent or for Easter, for christenings or weddings, for harvest time or Christmas. The modern affluent-puritan may claim the buttered loaf is an unnecessary extravagance, but for anyone who feels that life is lean enough, these breads make a simple life feel less harsh and more enjoyable.

Sweet butter dough

This is a very simple, very useful butter dough that is handy to make when you have a glut of summer fruit and you need to produce lots of baked goods quickly, such as the apple and custard loaf on page 120. You do need to cover the dough snugly while it sits in the refrigerator overnight, as the high fat content makes it remarkably good at picking up the flavors of other foods nearby. Mine once had the strange taste of smoked sausage. When this is unexpected, it's not so good.

2½ tsp fresh yeast, crumbled (4%)
1 medium egg (12%)
2 medium egg yolks (12%)
½ cup (125g) superfine sugar (25%)
4 cups (500g) soft white flour (100%)

7oz (200g) white leaven (40%)
(see pages 25–7)
½ cup (125g) light cream (25%)
1¼ tsp fine sea salt (2%)
¾ cup (175g) unsalted butter (35%)

Crumble the yeast and beat with the egg, egg yolks, and 1 tbsp sugar. Mix in all the remaining ingredients except the butter and knead roughly. Cover and leave for 10 minutes.

Slice the butter into thin pieces, then allow it to soften. Spread the pieces on top of the dough and work them roughly into it. Rub 1 tsp corn or olive oil on the work-surface and knead the dough on the oiled surface for 5 minutes, until the butter is combined and the dough is smooth. Knead the dough into a ball, then place it in a large, tightly-covered container that allows it room to rise, and keep it in the refrigerator.

Use the dough the following day, or at least 18 hours later.

Flaky butter buns

Bread dough layered with good, sweet butter is a constant in the baking traditions of northern Europe. Butter can slow down the rising process, and a way to add richness without losing speed is to layer the butter through the dough rather than kneading it in. This means the fat does not coat the grains of flour and so prevent yeast from accessing sugars to ferment, which is what causes the dough to rise. This is a slow dough, made over two days, weakening the flour and resulting in a tender crumb. On the first day, the dough is mixed, kneaded lightly, and kept in the refrigerator overnight. On the second, the dough is rolled with the butter and made into shapes which are left to rise and then baked.

TIP Let the butter buns rise overnight in the refrigerator, then bake them fresh on a Saturday or Sunday morning. You can also freeze them unbaked, although I've only tried keeping them in the freezer for a week.

3⅔ cups (500g) bread flour (100%)
1½ tsp fine sea salt (2%)
1¼ scant cups (275g) milk at 68°F (55%)
2 tsp fresh yeast, crumbled (2%)
¾ cup (175g) unsalted butter (35%)

In a bowl, combine the flour and salt. In another bowl or pitcher, beat together the milk and yeast. Pour the liquid in with the dry ingredients and mix with your hands until you have a firm dough. Scrape any remaining dough from your fingers into the bowl, cover with a cloth, and leave for 10 minutes.

Rub 1 tsp of corn or olive oil on the work-surface and knead the dough on the oiled surface for 10 seconds, ending with a smooth, round ball. Clean and dry the bowl, then rub lightly with a tsp of oil. Return the dough to the bowl and leave for 10 minutes. Remove the dough and knead once more on the oiled surface, returning the shape of the dough to a smooth, round ball. Cover the dough and place in the refrigerator overnight.

The following day, remove the dough from the refrigerator, and leave covered at room temperature (68°F) for 1 hour to lose some of its chill. Remove the butter from the refrigerator, and let that soften to something like the consistency of the dough. On a floured work-surface, roll out the dough until it is a ½in-thick rectangle. Cut the butter into thin slices and lay it out over two-thirds of the dough. Fold the remaining third back over to cover half the butter, then fold the dough over to cover that. All the butter should now be wrapped up inside the dough. Check that the dough is lightly floured on both sides, then roll out carefully until it is ½in thick again. Fold the dough in by thirds again, then cover it with a cloth and leave in a cool place for 1 hour.

Roll out the dough once more, but this time fold it in by quarters. The way to do this is by folding each end in so that they meet in the center, then folding these sides on top of each other (this is called a book fold). Cover the dough and leave to rest in a cool place for another hour.

To shape the buns, roll the dough out to a ½in-thick rectangle on a floured surface. Cut circles from the dough measuring about 4in in diameter, and pull the edges in toward the center, pinching them down to get a round or oval bun shape. Place smooth-side-up on a baking sheet lined with non-stick parchment paper. Cover with a cloth and leave to rise for 1½ hours in a warm (70–77°F) place.

Preheat the oven to 400°F. Bake the butter buns in the center of the oven for 25 minutes, or until crisp and a light brown in color. Allow to cool on the tray.

I like to eat these warm, stuffed with a piece of crisp bacon, or you could eat them with honey.

Italy

Italy is a country that I grew up with, from my early teens to my 20s. At the age of 15, I spent a winter in the small Lombardy town of Castellanza, with a family who struggled to get some of the Italian language into my head. Then later, as a photographer in the 1980s, I traveled back and forth, working here and there for a fashion magazine that was based in Milan. My Italian improved, but perhaps not as fast as my affection for the country and its people.

It was Wendy Fogarty, the founder of the British part of the Slow Food movement and an early activist for good bread in Britain, who nudged me to spend some more time in Turin. She'd guide me, prodding me to think about the provenance of the ingredients we bake with, and reminding me of the duty that we bakers have to promote considerate and sustainable agriculture.

To strengthen her argument, Wendy would sit me with young Italians who'd become politicized by the damage they saw in their countryside. Their arguments were both heartfelt and alarming. For me, Wendy, Turin, and the Slow Food movement set an example for the way that life could be. Since then, I have become deeply fond of the city, and it is where I now feel most at home in the world.

A few years later, in 2000, with the help of Giovanni Gai from the *Associazione Panificatori Artigiani* (the organization for artisan bakers in Turin) and of the Flour Advisory Bureau in London, I took a group of British bakers to run a small local bakery for the duration of the Slow Food *Salone del Gusto*. We used British flour as well as flour from the artisanal Mulino Marino in Cossano Belbo. We wanted both to learn and to bake together, with no competitive edge and no intention of Union

THIS PAGE, TOP TO BOTTOM: *rubatà chierese*, a *grissini*, at Marta Bera's shop; left to right, their assistant with Marta, Bruna, and their sister; doors in a Turin street; a plaited loaf and a *pane nero* made with rye flour and farro from Marta's shop in Turin's Via San Tommaso. OPPOSITE, CLOCKWISE FROM TOP LEFT: *pane carasau* from Antonio Mura in Buddusò, Sardinia; the dining room at Antiche Sera; Anna Maria of Antiche Sera with her son, Danielle; the interior of Latteria Bera Bruna; *pane di colomba*, a sweet Easter bread; *stirato Torinese*; *pane di mais*; *pane di olio*; bread at Marta's shop; discs of rosemary and rock salt flatbread called *croccante romana*. CENTER, CLOCKWISE FROM LEFT: Bruna and a bottle of whey; fresh cheese at Turin's central market; pastry chef Toni Vitiello.

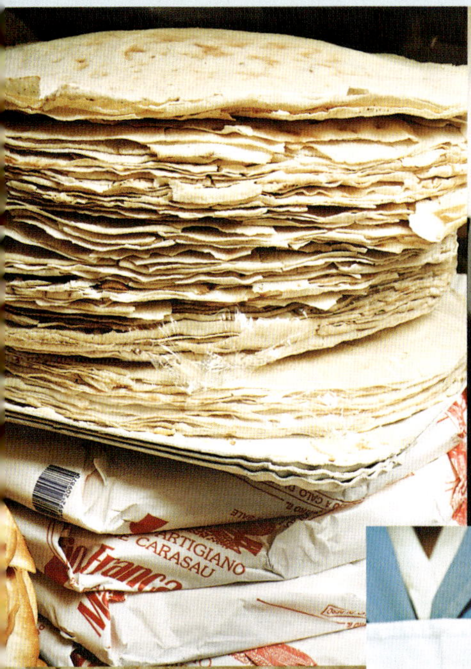
ARTIGIANO
CARASAU

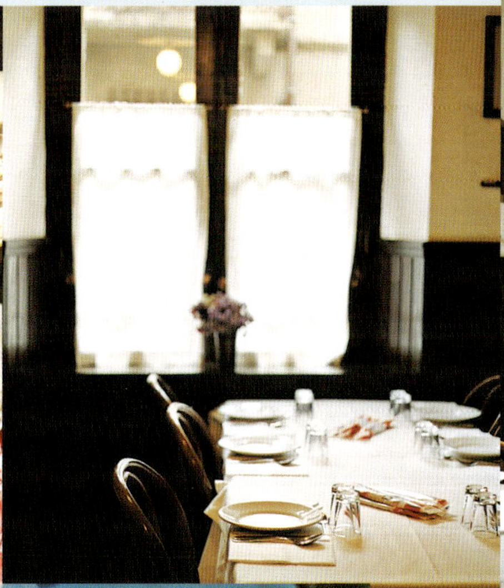

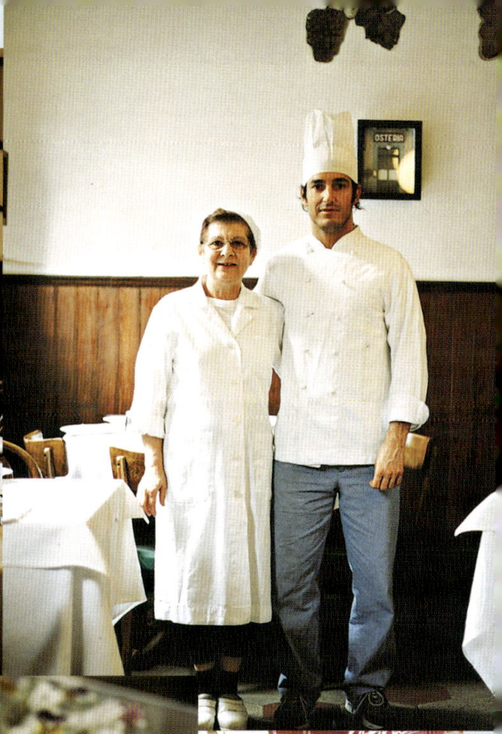

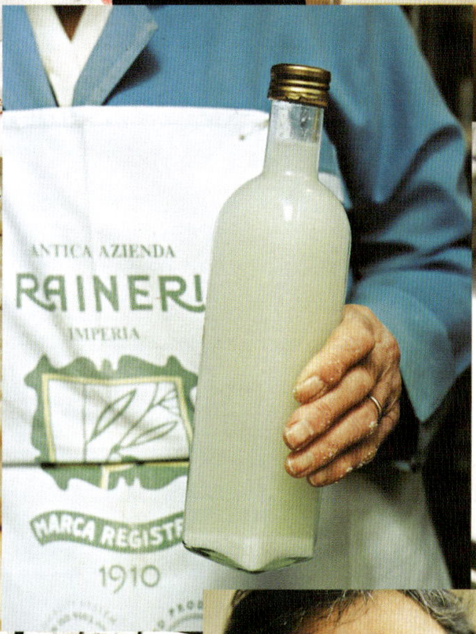
ANTICA AZIENDA
RAINERI
IMPERIA
MARCA REGISTR
1910

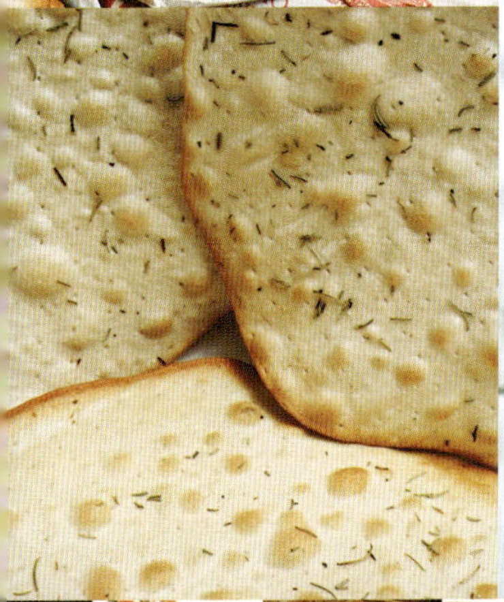

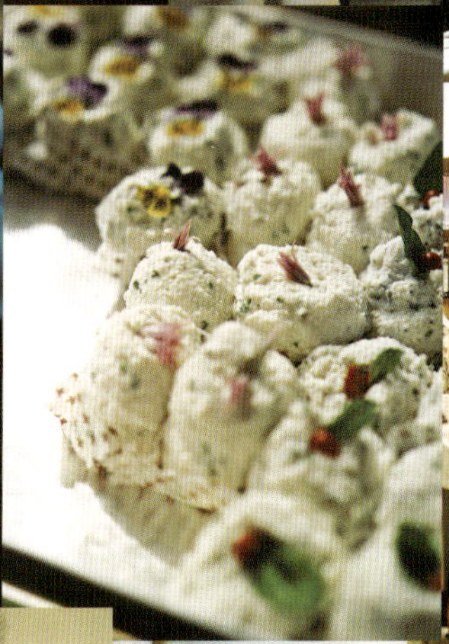

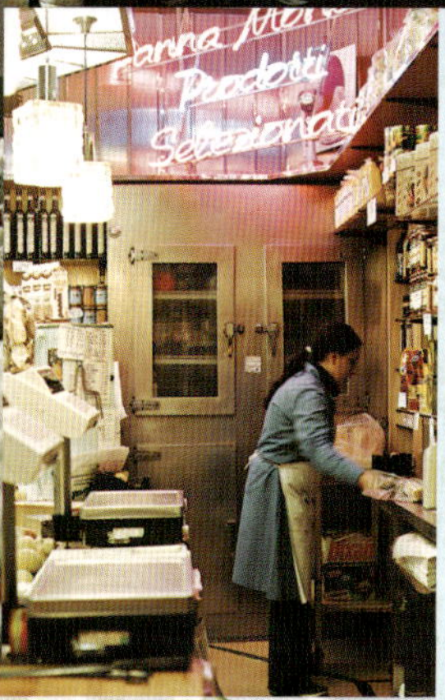
Prodotti
Selezionati

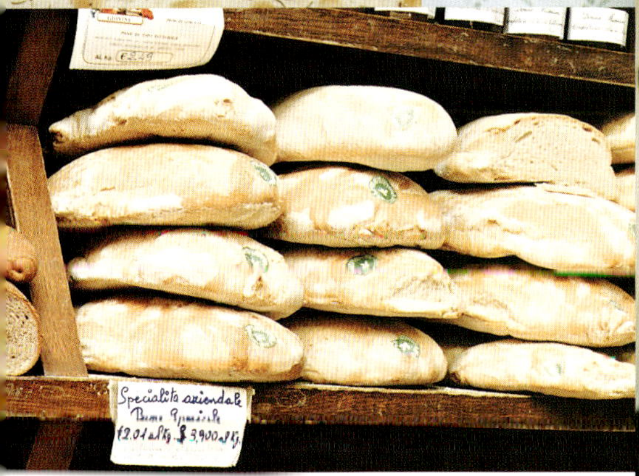

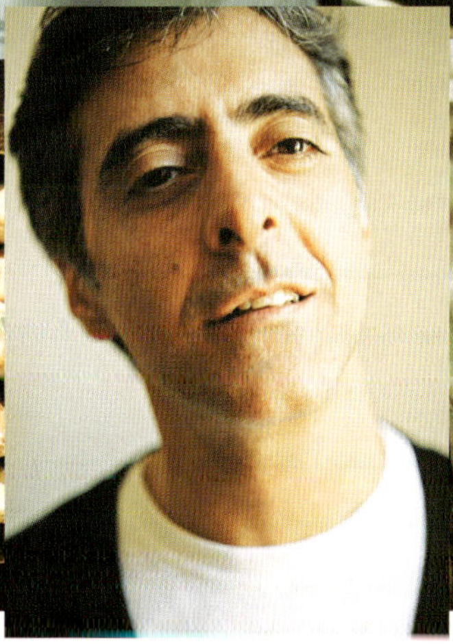

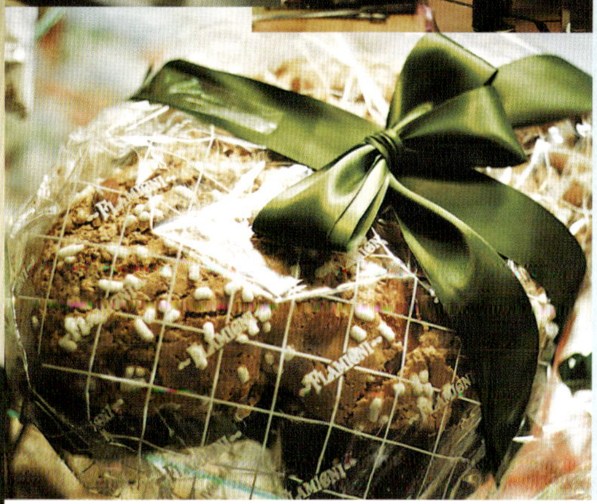

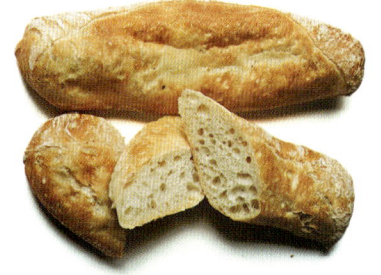

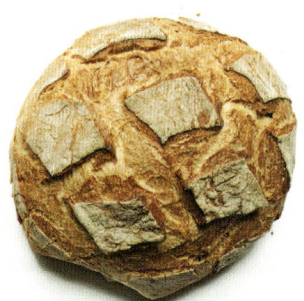

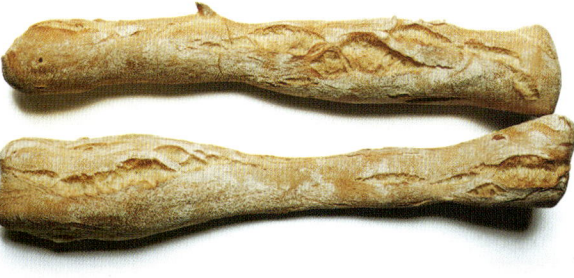

> "There was a time when simple flatbreads such as farinata and the Tuscan castagnaccio were sold by immigrant street vendors in Turin."

LEFT TO RIGHT: wedges of freshly baked *farinata*; the baker Stella with a tray of *farinata* at Focacceria Tipica Ligure, Turin; chickpea flour batter being poured into a hot baking dish.

Jack waving. It was a period of intense learning and hard work, and marked all of us in one way or another. But subsequently I have returned to Turin often, aided by my pastry chef friend Toni Vitiello, who has been my sturdy guide to excellent breads and baking in the city.

Italian bread is typified by the characteristics of the regional flour, though the "*doppio zero*" rating on each bag is not quite as definitive and helpful as it sounds. When I was working at a small artisan bakery in Milan, I noticed that the baker used two "00" flours. When I asked why, he said, "Well, one is a strong '00' and the other a soft '00' flour." That threw me, as I had always believed that it was enough to simply get Italian "00" flour. It seems that flours vary widely in Italy and bakers there, as in any country, might use two or more flours blended in order to achieve a particular result. At Mulino Marino the flour was stoneground, organic and beige-colored, and produced beautiful bread with a sweet crust.

The success of a bakery is not simply due to the baker or their bread. The unsung heroes and heroines for every artisan baker are the men and women who sell the bread—those people who turn the experience of buying bread into something softly, or sometimes strictly, pleasurable. Toni Vitiello had insisted that I see the best bread and cheese shops in Turin. Here, three women have the market for bread and cheese stitched up: the Bera sisters. On Via San Tommaso are two shops, on either side of the road, run by the sisters. Two sisters run the Latteria Bera Bruna, which stocks an intensely regional selection of local cheeses, and the third sister, Marta, runs the Panetteria Bera, where most of the fine loaves, *grissini*, and crisp breads from Piedmont and elsewhere in Italy can be found. It was Bruna, the eldest sister, who first welcomed me at the Latteria years ago, when I was sourcing whey that I could use while I baked there.

At Marta's Panetteria, the stars are the *grissini* and crisp breads. There are the *grissino stirato del Torinese*, pale golden in color because of the malt, olive oil, and *lardo*, or pork fat, made with soft bread dough that is cut thin and stretched to elongate the aeration. And there are the tightly hand-rolled *rubatà chierese*, pale and almost white, made from a tender cookie dough that crunches to a powdery crumb.

In every restaurant or *osteria* (the Italian name for a tavern), sticks of either or both *grissini* will sit in the center of the table. At the Osteria Antiche Sera, one of the best places to taste artisan Piedmont ingredients, Anna Maria and her son Danielle serve the most exquisitely blunt and honest food I have ever eaten, and bread is very much part of the set table. Little bags of crisp *grissini rubatà* sit in the center of every table, alongside a basket of simple white bread. These are the breads that are eaten with the paper-thin *lardo*, herb-cured lard served on its own, or the soft mountain goat's cheese topped with *salsa verde*.

The Ligurian *farinata* is still sold at a few places in the city. I visit one small bakery where round metal platters are heated and filled with a batter made from chickpea flour, water, salt, and olive oil. After barely 10 minutes in the hot oven the *farinata* emerge, crisp on the surface but almost custard-soft underneath.

There was a time when simple flatbreads such as *farinata* and the Tuscan *castagnaccio*, made from chestnuts, were sold by immigrant street vendors in Turin. Metal pans filled with hot coals were topped with a griddle on which the bread would be cooked. These vendors were typical in Turin through the early 1900s, until the pizza started to gain popularity in the north of Italy. Today, there are very few vendors of these early flatbreads left, and the pizza from Napoli is everywhere. Tastes change, and in the space of a generation some popular traditions can almost be lost.

Olive oil flatbread

1⅓ cups (330g) water at 68°F (66%)
7oz (200g) white leaven (40%)
  (see pages 25–27)
1 tsp ground malt powder (1%)
5 tbsp (80g) extra virgin olive oil (16%)
1¼ tsp fresh yeast, crumbled (1%)
3⅔ cups (500g) bread flour (100%)
1½ tsp fine sea salt (2%)

There are bakeries in Genoa that produce this sort of flatbread, known as focaccia. The name is now synonymous with the bubbly, open-textured bread that has become a regular feature in artisan bakeries from San Francisco to London, but seldom is this texture seen in Italy. Usually, the bread is simply made with the house white dough, and it is the shape that defines it. Contemporary artisan bakers work the dough over many hours, so that holes created by the fermenting yeast are stretched and enlarged, giving an exaggerated honeycomb effect. I was always convinced that the texture relied on high-speed mixing, the sort only really possible in commercial bakeries. But, as the bread in the picture shows, it can be made by hand, and simply folded every hour to give this effect. What enhances it, if anything, is a hot oven.

In a bowl or pitcher, beat the water with the leaven, malt powder, 2 tbsp of the olive oil, and yeast until the mixture is smooth. In another bowl, combine the flour with the salt. Pour the liquid into the dry ingredients and mix them with your hands until you have a soft, sticky dough. Scrape any remaining dough from your fingers into the bowl, cover with a cloth, and leave for 10 minutes.

Tip the remaining olive oil onto a lipped tray and rub it so that the tray is coated. Knead the dough on the tray lightly for 10 seconds, then flip it over so you get a round ball. Cover the dough and leave for an additional 10 minutes. Knead the dough on the oiled tray once more, returning the shape of the dough to a smooth, round ball. Place it back in the bowl, cover, and leave for 1 hour in a warm (70–77°F) place.

Rub 1 tsp corn or olive oil onto the work-surface. Pat the dough out into a rectangle on the oiled surface, and fold it in by thirds each way. Flip the dough over so that the seam faces downward. Cover, and then repeat this patting out and folding every 40 minutes for the next 2 hours. Each time you are gently stretching and folding the dough rather than punching it to knock out the gas. It is important to check that the temperature of the dough does not rise above 70–77°F; it should always feel cool to the touch. When the dough is ready, a cut into the center should reveal a dramatic network of holes.

Lightly oil two 12 x 8in baking sheets. Cut the dough into two equal pieces, and place each seam-side-down in the center of a sheet, then dimple the surface with your fingertips to slightly flatten it. Don't worry that the dough is only sitting in the center. Cover the dough and leave for 15 minutes, ideally in a warmer place near the oven at 77–82°F.

Preheat the oven to 425°F. Uncover the dough and stretch it out so that it covers more of the sheet. To do this, lift the dough at each side and pull it out toward the edge of the sheet as far as it will go. I usually cover the dough again at this point and leave it for an additional 10 minutes before stretching it one last time to fully cover the sheet. Drizzle a little olive oil and sprinkle coarse sea salt over the surface, then make deep impressions with your fingertips pressing down into the dough right to the sheet.

Bake the bread in the center of the oven for 35 minutes, or until the upper surface is a good golden brown. Using a spatula, ease the bread from the sheet and let it cool on a wire rack.

Soft curd loaf

Fresh cheese, made from the curd strained from whole milk (see page 45) can be crumbled into the mixing liquid and used to enrich and fatten the crumb of the loaf. This loaf can make use of other crumbly cheeses such as Cheshire or Wensleydale. If it is summer and you have too many chives, finely chop a handful and add these to the dough.

1¼ cups (300g) water at 68°F (60%)
2 tsp fresh yeast, crumbled (2%)
½ cup (125g) soft curd cheese, eg ricotta (25%)
2 cups (250g) all-purpose flour (50%)
1¾ cups (250g) bread flour (50%)
1½ tsp fine sea salt (2%)

In a bowl or pitcher, beat together the water, yeast, and curd cheese. In a large bowl, combine the two flours with the salt. Pour the liquid into the dry ingredients and stir until you have a soft, sticky dough.

Rub 1 tsp of corn or olive oil onto the work-surface and knead the dough on the oiled surface for 10 seconds, ending with a smooth, round ball. Clean and dry the bowl, then rub lightly with a tsp of oil. Return the dough to the bowl and leave for an additional 10 minutes. Remove the dough and knead once more on the oiled surface, returning the shape of the dough to a smooth, round ball. Place it back in the bowl, cover, and leave for 1 hour in a warm (70–77°F) place.

Grease and flour a deep 4½ x 7½in loaf pan. Shape the loaf into a baton (see page 21). Lower it neatly into the prepared pan, then cover with a cloth and allow to rise for 1½ hours, or until almost doubled in height.

Preheat the oven to 410°F. Dust the top of the loaf with flour and bake for 15 minutes, then lower the heat to 350°F and bake for an additional 25–30 minutes, or until the top of the loaf is a shiny dark brown and the loaf has come away from the sides of the pan. Remove from the pan and cool on a wire rack.

Chickpea pancakes

My friend Toni Vitiello, a very good pastry chef from Turin, took me to his favorite bakery one afternoon to eat *farinata* with him. *Farinata* is a traditional Ligurian pancake made with chickpea flour and olive oil, from the same school as the English Yorkshire pudding and almost identical to the Provençal *socca*. So this baker removed great trays covered in the blistered yellow flatbread (the sulfurous color comes from both the chickpea flour and the olive oil) from the oven and cut wedges for us before wrapping them in sheets of paper. I would be lying if I said I loved my first mouthful; I spat it into the bin. "What? This was the food I grew up on!" said Toni. So I ate another piece and another. Now every time I go back, I buy more *farinata* and I'm halfway through my training and getting close to loving it.

1⅔ cups (200g) chickpea flour (100%)
¾ cup (200g) water at 68°F (100%)
½ tsp fine sea salt (1%)
3 tbsp (50g) olive oil (25%)
2 tbsp olive oil for frying
a small sprig of rosemary, chopped

In a bowl, beat together the flour, water, and salt until you have a smooth batter. Cover and leave for 2 hours.

Preheat the oven to 425°F. Add the olive oil to the batter and beat well until combined. Take a large, flat pan, such as a *paella* pan, and add the 2 tbsp of olive oil. Heat this on top of the stove until the oil is smoking, then sprinkle in the rosemary. Let this sizzle for a moment, then pour in the batter. Remove the pan from the heat, place it in the hot oven, then shut the door and leave for 20 minutes. By this time the pancake should be slightly puffed and lightly brown on top.

Remove the *farinata* from the oven, let it cool in the pan for a moment, then put it on a cutting board and cut into squares or wedges to spread with something like tapenade, or serve with a bowl of good olives and a Negroni.

Sage, cheese, and shallot pie

Sometimes bread can encase the meal. In this recipe, whole shallots are baked in the oven and then allowed to cool before being halved and mixed with melted butter, chopped sage, and cheese. This mixture is baked between two discs of bread dough to make a substantial supper dish. I like adding cubes of cooked beets when it is in season, as their earthy taste adds vigor to the loaf. The olive oil dough used in this recipe is the same as for the flatbread on page 151. Simply halve all the quantities to produce around 1¼lb (550g) of dough, and follow the mixing and kneading instructions in the first two paragraphs of that recipe, so that you have a smooth ball of dough which has rested for 1 hour.

FOR THE FILLING:

12 medium shallots, unpeeled (43%)
¼ cup (50g) unsalted butter (9%)
a dozen sage leaves (0.5%)
9oz (250g) good goat cheese (45%)
fine sea salt and ground black pepper

FOR THE DOUGH:

1¼lb (550g) olive oil dough (100%) (see page 151 and recipe introduction note)

Preheat the oven to 350°F. Place the shallots on a baking sheet and roast for 40 minutes, or until a knife pierces the flesh easily. To conserve fuel, I like to do this when the oven is on for another purpose, such as cooking the supper. Leave the shallots in the refrigerator overnight for use the following day.

Carefully peel the tough brown outer layers of skin from the cold shallots, leaving the tender, purple-ish bulbs. Cut these in half. Melt the butter and mix with the shallots, the sage (torn into pieces), and the goat cheese (chopped into rough cubes). Place this to one side while you roll out the dough.

Rub 1 tsp of olive oil onto the work-surface. Divide the dough into two equal pieces and, on the oiled surface, roll each into a 16 x 8in oval. Place one of these on a suitably sized oiled baking sheet. Spread the shallot mixture evenly over the base, season with salt and pepper, then lay the other piece of dough on top. Seal it well at the edges, then press the top sheet of dough down at several points across its surface to seal it to the base. Using a sharp knife, cut five or six air vents in the top of the dough for steam to escape. Lightly cover the pie with a cloth and leave for 40 minutes.

Preheat the oven to 425°F. Bake in the center of the oven for 40 minutes, or until the bread is crisp and golden. Either serve hot or leave until warm—but this pie is best eaten before it gets cold.

Brown butter picklets

1 scant cup (100g) whole-wheat flour (50%)
¾ cup (100g) all-purpose flour (50%)
½ tsp fine sea salt (1%)
6 tbsp (100g) milk at 68°F (50%)
6 tbsp (100g) water at 68°F (50%)
¾ tsp fresh yeast, crumbled (2%)
¼ cup (50g) butter (25%)
1 tsp baking soda (2.5%)
1 tbsp extra water (8%)
oil, lard, or butter for frying

In a bowl, combine the white and whole-wheat flours with the salt. In another bowl, mix the milk and water with the yeast. Pour the liquid into the dry ingredients, then beat well until smooth. Cover the bowl and leave for 2 hours, until the mixture is bubbly.

Place the butter in a saucepan and heat until it is nut-brown, then remove the pan from the heat and pour the butter into a small bowl to cool slightly and stop cooking. (You could simply run cold water across the underside of the pan to lower the heat quickly.) Beat the browned butter into the yeasted batter until it is evenly combined. Mix the soda with the 1 tbsp of water and stir into the batter.

Preheat a non-stick skillet, and in it heat 1 tsp of oil, lard, or butter until it is almost smoking hot. Rub this evenly around the surface with a ball of paper towel. Lower the heat and put 1–2 tbsp of batter into the pan per picklet, cooking two or three in the pan at a time. Cook until the edges are crisp and brown and the surface is broken with air bubbles that break through to the base of the pan—a minute or so. Using a spatula, loosen each picklet from the skillet and flip over. Cook each picklet for another minute, or until both sides are brown. Remove from the pan, place on a plate, and cover with a cloth while you cook the remaining picklets.

My mother had a large aluminum electric skillet called a Sunbeam, which used to be brought out every Saturday to make pikelets, what I knew to be tiny pancakes made with milk, egg, and butter. But there is an earlier version, almost forgotten now, with the slightly different spelling of "picklet," which was a version of the crumpet. This was a leavened bread cooked on a griddle and served warm with a little butter or jelly.

Garlic and goose fat pancakes

These little pancakes, made with cooked potato, goose fat, and garlic, can be stacked on a plate and served with crisp herring roes and a glass of something good. They are best made and eaten quickly, though they can be wrapped in foil and placed in a hot oven to reheat.

½ cup (50g) millet flour (50%)
½ cup (50g) all-purpose flour (50%)
½ tsp fine sea salt (3%)
3½oz (100g) cooked potato, sieved (100%)
½ cup (125g) water at 68°F (125%)
½ tsp fresh yeast, crumbled (3%)
2 tbsp goose fat or lard (30%)
1 clove garlic, cut into slivers
2 tbsp chopped parsley

In a large bowl, combine the two flours with the salt. In another bowl or pitcher beat the sieved potato with the water and yeast. Pour the liquid into the dry ingredients, mixing well until you have a smooth, thick batter. Leave at room temperature for 2 hours, or until frothy.

In a saucepan, heat the goose fat and garlic over a low heat for 2–3 minutes so that the garlic barely browns. Pour this into the batter, stirring well so that the oil does not get a chance to cook the mixture. Stir in the parsley.

Preheat a non-stick skillet, and in it heat 1 tsp of oil, lard, or butter until it is almost smoking hot. Rub this evenly around the surface with a ball of paper towel. Lower the heat and put 1 tbsp of batter into the pan per pancake, cooking three or four in the pan at a time. Cook until the edges are crisp and brown and the surface is broken with air bubbles that break through to the base of the pan—about a minute. Using a spatula, loosen each pancake from the skillet and flip over. Cook each pancake for another minute, or until both sides are brown. Remove from the pan, place on a plate, and cover with a cloth while you cook the remaining pancakes.

Lard cake

There are many versions of this famous bread made with lard or clarified dripping. Some contain currants or golden raisins, but the version here is simpler. Susan Beaty-Pownall, who edited a series of cookbooks for *Queen* magazine in the early 20th century, gives a recipe for lard cake which simply uses lard and sugar. To my taste, this plain cake is more adaptable and I would serve it with something like figs or rum-soaked currants.

TIP Buy your lard from a good butcher and try to insist that it is unadulterated pork lard, which has a much better flavor than the cheap blocks.

3⅗ cups (500g) bread flour (100%)
1½ tsp fine sea salt (2%)
7oz (200g) white leaven (40%) (see pages 25–27)
1 cup (250g) water at 68°F (50%)
2½ tsp fresh yeast, crumbled (2%)
¾ cup (150g) pork lard (30%)
⅔ cup (150g) superfine sugar (30%)
scraping of nutmeg
2 tbsp superfine sugar for dredging

In a large bowl, combine the flour and the salt. In another bowl or pitcher, beat together the leaven, water, and yeast. Pour the liquid into the dry ingredients and stir until you have a soft, sticky dough. Scrape any remaining dough from your fingers into the bowl, cover and leave for 10 minutes.

Rub 1 tsp of corn or olive oil onto the work-surface and knead the dough on the oiled surface for 10 seconds, ending with a smooth, round ball. Clean and dry the bowl, then rub with a tsp of oil. Return the dough to the bowl, cover, and leave for an additional 10 minutes. Remove the dough, knead once more on the oiled surface, returning the shape of the dough to a smooth, round ball. Place it back in the bowl, cover, and leave for 1 hour in a warm (70–77°F) place.

On a floured work-surface, roll the dough out until it is a ½in-thick rectangle. Cut the lard into thin slices and lay it out over two-thirds of the dough. Sprinkle the sugar evenly over the lard, then fold the remaining third of the dough back over to cover half the lard, then fold the dough over to cover that. All of the lard and sugar should now be wrapped up inside the dough. Check that the dough is lightly floured on both sides, then roll the dough out carefully until it is again a ½in-thick rectangle. Fold the dough in by thirds once more, then cover it with a cloth and leave in a cool place for 30 minutes.

Roll the dough out on the work-surface until it is again about a 1cm-thick rectangle. Roll the dough up from one end into a tight cylinder, then leave it to sit on the work-surface, covered, for 10 minutes.

Line a 10in spring-form cake pan (or a similar ovenproof pan) with non-stick parchment paper. Using a sharp knife, cut through the cylinder of dough lengthwise. Then, with the cut surface facing upward, spiral the dough around. Working carefully, as this is a bit tricky, lift this spiral and plonk it down inside the pan, cut-side-upward. Cover the pan and leave the dough in a warm (77°F) place for 1 hour, or until almost doubled in height.

Preheat the oven to 400°F. Sprinkle the nutmeg over the surface, then dredge the upper surface with 2 tbsp of superfine sugar. Bake in the center of the oven for 20 minutes, then reduce the heat to 350°F and bake for an additional 40 minutes, or until the top is a good dark brown, verging on burnt. Allow the cake to cool in the pan for 15 minutes before carefully transferring it to a wire rack to cool. Wrap in waxed paper to store.

THE FAT OF THE LAND | ENGLAND

England

A food writer once complained bitterly to me about bread in England. It was an opinion colored by one visit, one city, and one baker, as if a stop-over tourist had judged British food by the restaurants at Heathrow. There is good bread in England, but it isn't celebrated and we're not self-congratulatory by habit. You just need to know where to look.

In London there's Troels Bendix at Breadsetcetera in Wandsworth, Gail Stephen's standard setting Baker & Spice in Knightsbridge and Queen's Park, Sally Clarke's eponymous bakery in Notting Hill, partners Rachel Duffield and Liz Weisberg at the Lighthouse bakery near Clapham Junction, Matt Jones at Flourpower in Dulwich, and Manuel Monade and his wood-fired Llopis oven at Born & Bread in Peckham. Outside London, there's the Café Royal Bakery in Newcastle, Hobbs House Bakery in Chipping Sodbury, and Peter Cook at S. C. Price and Sons in Ludlow. And there are many more making good bread quietly, without fanfare or even much local praise.

Bridport, a beautiful town near the west Dorset coast, is the home of Leakers. Aidan Chapman's bakery is situated behind a narrow high-street store front, with windows along one side so that the bakery is lit by the morning sun rising. Running back along the right-hand wall is an old deck oven, once oil-fired but now run with electricity. Every morning this oven produces leaven breads, crusty top-split tin loaves to make a fine English sandwich, semolina-crusted cobs, "winter warmers" made with local ale and hard cheese, egg-glazed Bath buns, and yeast pastries layered with local farm butter. It's early morning and a queue has formed already, mostly of customers who know exactly what they want and how it should be baked.

THIS PAGE FROM TOP RIGHT: an old millstone at Cann Mill, Dorset; Jack Lang holds a 100 percent leaven bread, fresh from his wood-fired home oven. LEFT: baker Emmanuel Hadjiandreou holds a barrel of leaven flutes at Daylesford Farm Shop, Gloucestershire. OPPOSITE PAGE, CLOCKWISE FROM TOP LEFT: 32kg sacks of stone-milled flour at Cann Mill; two rye breads rise in linen-lined baskets on Lang's kitchen table; miller Michael Stoate; Lang's loaves cooling next to a bowl of English butter; the knobbly top of a grain loaf coming out of Lang's oven; pizza-making in the garden; Cann Mills' office sign. CENTER: a thick layer of fragrant thyme growing on the warm roof of Lang's oven.

> "A growing number of bakers... [are] keen to develop baking methods to suit locally grown grain."

I ask Aidan about the provenance of his ingredients. "We have a farmer around the corner who supplies our vegetables, pears, and the soft loganberries for these tarts," he says. "We use a local cider for our apple rye bread, and the same ciderman supplies the apples for our tarts. Customers also bring in fruit from their garden, and we give them some of whatever we make from it in return."

Like a growing number of bakers in Britain, Aidan sees the flour he uses as intrinsic to the flavor and character of the loaf and is keen to develop baking methods to suit locally grown grain and turn the resulting flour into a perfect loaf. Such loaves have a different crumb and crust to ones made with imported flour, and a beauty all of their own.

The greatest impact on artisan baking in England over the last 20 years has come from millers such as John Lister at Shipton Mill, Michael and Clare Marriage at Doves Farm, and first Norman Stoate and now his son Michael at Cann Mills. They have given practical support to organic farmers by buying and milling their grain, and have made available flour from locally grown, unusual, and historic varieties of cereal. Their dedicated work has found its champions in a new generation of bakers.

At Daylesford in Gloucestershire, baker Emmanuel Hadjiandreou is working with Michael Stoate, who mills their harvest of Hereward and Maris Widgeon wheat, so that the loaves come from the surrounding land. "We were growing wheat for cow feed," says Emmanuel, "and I said: 'Why don't we try growing wheat for milling?' Though the farmer was very doubtful, we had a sample of Hereward milled and it produced a great loaf—nutty, sweet, heavy, but not doughy." Along with the bakery and farm store, Daylesford includes a creamery producing award-winning cheeses, a greengrocer, a butcher, and a small dining hall, all using produce from two local estates. This well-funded endeavor is just what you might hope for from a local government initiative but is, instead, supported by the efforts of one family: the Bamfords.

Like the artisan on the high street, many home-bakers like going after excellence and a primitive baking experience: grinding the wheat for freshly milled flour, nursing a natural starter through its infancy to full-blown fermentation, and blending grains and flours to create a personal mix. Jack Lang, "Entrepreneur in Residence" at the University of Cambridge, is a passionate baker down to the wood-fired oven in his garden. "Traditional wood-fired ovens are good at maintaining steady, even heat, and are economical," says Jack. "Equally, naturally leavened breads are easy to manage, especially for the home-baker, as the dough matures more slowly and the point when the loaf gets to the oven is less critical."

LEFT TO RIGHT: baker Aidan Chapman holding his rye and local cider loaf; Aidan and trainee Caroline Rouiller standing outside the bakery in Bridport, Dorset.

White loaf with grated chestnuts

The large amount of fat left over when you roast a duck or goose has traditionally been used to enrich other foods, preserve meats, and even sipped by the warm spoonful to ease congestion. It was used, and not wasted. In this recipe, shallots are softened in duck fat, then stirred into the dough with grated chestnuts.

TIP You can substitute vacuum-packed cooked whole chestnuts, available all year round, for the freshly toasted chestnuts in the recipe.

⅓ cup (75g) duck fat (15%)
2 small shallots, finely chopped (6%)
1⅓ cups (200g) fresh chestnuts, roasted, peeled and finely grated (40%)
3⅔ cups (500g) bread flour (100%)
1½ tsp fine sea salt (2%)
1¼ cups (300g) water at 68°F (60%)
1¼ tsp fresh yeast, crumbled (1%)
7oz (200g) rye leaven (40%) (see pages 25–27 and 31)

Melt the duck fat in a saucepan, then cook the finely chopped shallots in the fat until they begin to sizzle. Lower the heat, cover with a lid, and cook for 5 minutes, or until the shallots have softened and become almost translucent. Remove from the heat, stir in the chestnuts and allow to cool until warm.

In a bowl, combine the flour with the salt. In another bowl or pitcher, mix the water with the yeast and rye leaven. Add the liquid to the dry ingredients and stir with your hands until you have a soft, sticky dough. Scrape any remaining dough from your fingers into the bowl, cover and leave for 10 minutes. Add the chestnut and shallot mixture, squidging it well into the dough with your fingers to mix it as evenly as possible. Cover the dough again and leave for an additional 10 minutes.

Rub 1 tsp of corn or olive oil on the work-surface and knead the dough on the oiled surface for 10 seconds, ending with a smooth, round ball. Clean and dry the bowl, then rub lightly with a tsp of oil. Return the dough to the bowl and leave for an additional 10 minutes. Remove the dough and knead once more on the oiled surface, returning the dough to the shape of a smooth, round ball. Place it back in the bowl, cover, and leave for 1 hour in a warm (70–77°F) place.

Dust two dishtowels with rye flour, and line two 8 x 4in oblong loaf pans with these. They will act as the rising baskets (or use flour-dusted wicker baskets, if you have them). Divide the dough into two equal pieces. Shape each piece into a baton (see page 21) and sit it seam-side-up inside the cloth. Cover the upper surface with another cloth and allow to rise for 2 hours.

Preheat the oven to 425°F. Carefully up-turn the loaves onto a flour-dusted baking sheet and, using a sharp blade, slash the dough diagonally two or three times. Bake in the center of the oven for 45 minutes, until each loaf is a good rich brown color and sounds hollow when tapped on the bottom. Remove from the oven and allow to cool on a wire rack.

Fried flatbread with dill seeds and pork crackling

1¾ cups (250g) bread flour (100%)
¾ tsp fine sea salt (2%)
1 tsp dill seeds (2%)
⅔ cup (150g) water at 68°F (60%)
2 tsp fresh yeast, crumbled (2%)
3½oz (100g) soft pork crackling or rendered beef scraps, finely chopped (40%)
lard or dripping for brushing and frying

A good rib of beef will usually have some bits of slightly gristly fat, which don't completely render down, even after roasting. Likewise, the crackling on some cuts of pork will remain soft and chewy, rather than become the crisp, tasty accompaniment to a roast dinner. We might discard these scraps, but in Russia and the Ukraine I've seen home-cooks save them to use in a beet soup or when baking. This recipe is based on a traditional bread made for me by Farkhat and Saodat, a young Uzbek couple working in Moscow. They used beef fat, which gave the loaf a rich, meaty taste. As the dough is mixed cold, the rendered scraps won't release any extra fat until the bread is cooked. It makes an excellent thin bread, perfect with a boiled ham joint or a roast.

TIP You can make these rendered scraps at home by cutting the excess fat from a joint of pork or beef into small cubes and roasting them in the oven. This will also give you a bowl of dripping.

In a large bowl, roughly combine the flour, salt, and dill seeds. In another bowl or pitcher, beat the water with the yeast. Stir the liquid into the dry ingredients and mix with your hands until you have a soft, sticky dough. Mix the chopped crackling into the dough. Scrape any remaining dough from your fingers into the bowl, cover and leave for 10 minutes.

Rub 1 tsp of corn or olive oil onto the work-surface and knead the dough on the oiled surface for 10 seconds, ending with a smooth, round ball. Clean and dry the bowl, then rub lightly with a tsp of oil. Return the dough to the bowl and leave for an additional 10 minutes. Remove the dough and knead once more on the oiled surface, ending up with the dough in the shape of a smooth, round ball. Place it back in the bowl, cover, and leave for 1 hour in a warm (70–77°F) place.

Lightly flour the work-surface and roll the dough out into a 16 x 8in rectangle. Lightly brush the surface of the dough with melted lard, then cut the dough lengthwise into four strips, each measuring 16 x 2in. Roll one strip up tightly, then continue to roll the next strip where the last ended, continuing this rolling until all the strips have been used. Sit the coil of dough on its end and, using the ball of your hand, bash the coil flat. Check that it's not sticking, and dust underneath and over the dough with additional flour, then roll the dough out again, this time into a circle to cover the base of your skillet. Cover the dough on the work-surface and allow it to rise for 30 minutes.

Place 1 tbsp of lard in a wide, heavy skillet and leave it over a gentle heat to get hot. Carefully lower the disc of dough into the pan and fry it gently over a low heat. I use a heat diffuser ring over a low flame and move the pan onto this once the dough is in it—this stops the heat burning a spot in the center of the bread. With a pair of tongs, lift the edge of the dough after 2 minutes to make sure it is browning well but not burning. If it is browning too quickly, reduce the heat. After 4 minutes, flip the dough over and cook the other side for the same length of time. Once cooked, transfer the bread to a warm plate and serve.

The dry breads of winter

THE DRY BREADS OF WINTER | INTRODUCTION

Grain and flour are hard to store for long periods without damp and vermin turning them into something less palatable. Moist grains sprout during the wet winter months, flour molds or mildews, and soft breads stale and harden. But if the flour is made into breads rolled thin and baked crisp, the grain has been converted into food that stores well and is always ready to be eaten. As a primitive convenience food, the dry biscuit, cracker, and crisp bread once helped nourish communities through the long winter months until the spring, when the soil would again provide green food.

Today we make these breads because of their taste, their convenience, and the way in which they can combine with other foods. Often they are leavened with soda or yeast, creating a softer crunch. Though we now tend to judge flour by how well it can produce light, aerated bread, these traditional flatbreads only really work with the less glutinous flours that cannot produce elastic and resilient dough; if the flour is too strong, the result is leathery. Flours such as rye, barley, oat, and buckwheat make generously flavored crisp breads with a tender texture.

These breads are less demanding on our home ovens as they need a drier heat and don't need the explosive temperatures and steamy atmosphere that suit crusty, open-textured breads. Some, such as the oatcakes, are fully dried in the oven. Others, such as the dark crisp rye bread, might need crisping up before eating (just pop them in the toaster or a hot oven for a few minutes). All of them can be made simply by hand and require little more baking equipment than a flat metal baking sheet.

Dark crisp rye bread

Slightly salty, hard, and brittle, rye breads such as these were once the mainstay of life in Sweden. During World War II, these breads, called *knäckebröd*, were a dry ration supplied to soldiers. Sweden's most contemporary bakers still produce different versions. Starkly modern in appearance, such breads are very popular. One of the best artisan producers of *knäckebröd* is Robert Saberski's Roslagsbröd bakery in Gimo, north of Stockholm. Baker Leif Torstensson studiously watches over the yellow-painted machines chugging away as they stretch and roll the wet sticky dough into dimpled sheets, finally appearing as round discs with a hole in the middle. Traditionally, a pole was threaded through the hole to hang the breads by the fire to dry and crisp.

TIP I've used a little rye leaven in the mix, which gently sours the dough and emphasizes the natural tang of the rye flour. But it is more common to only use commercial yeast so, if you desire, leave the leaven out. Try altering the coarseness of the rye flour that you use. Stoneground rye, though difficult to work into a leavened rye bread, works well as a crisp rye bread.

¾ cup (200g) water at 68°F (100%)
½ tsp fresh yeast, crumbled (1%)
3½oz (100g) rye leaven (50%)
(see pages 25–27 and 31)
1⅔ cups (200g) fine or wholegrain rye flour (100%)
¾ tsp fine sea salt (2%)

In a bowl, beat together the water, yeast, and leaven. In another bowl, combine the flour and salt. Stir the dry ingredients into the yeasted mixture until you have a thick paste. Cover and leave for 3 hours, until the mixture has risen.

Tear a piece of parchment paper into two pieces, each large enough to cover a 12 x 8in baking sheet. Place one sheet of paper on the work-surface and scrape half of the batter onto it. Dredge the batter-dough heavily with rye flour and roll it out to ¼–⅓in thick, dusting the top of the dough with more rye flour should it even hint at sticking to the rolling pin. Transfer the dough-covered paper onto a baking sheet, then repeat with the other half of the mixture. Cover both sheets with a dry cloth and leave in a warm (73–82°F) place for about 2 hours, or until doubled in height.

Preheat the oven to 425°F. With the end of a pencil or a wooden spoon, stab at the surface of the rye dough to make dimples all over it. Repeat with the other sheet, then use a sharp knife to cut 4in squares in the dough. Bake each tray for 40–50 minutes, or until the upper surface is lightly tipped with golden patches against the gray rye crust.

Allow to cool on a wire rack overnight so that the rye breads become dry and brittle. Break into squares and pack into an airtight container.

Light rye flatbread

These round flatbreads, made with a combination of rye and white wheat flours, can be baked quickly and kept soft if covered with a cloth. This is how they would traditionally be made in Finland. Otherwise they can be made brittle, and more suited to dunking into a broth or a braise, by leaving them in the oven for 15 minutes longer.

TIP After baking for 20 minutes, the flatbreads can be removed from the oven and quickly split with a serrated knife, then returned to the hot oven to crisp. This turns the breads into thin rusks, good to serve with cured fish, marinated vegetables, or cream cheeses.

2 cups (300g) bread flour (75%)
1 scant cup (100g) fine rye flour (25%)
1 tsp fine sea salt (2%)
1¼ cups (300g) water at 68°F (75%)
1½ tsp fresh yeast, crumbled (1.5%)
3 tsp honey (3%)

In a bowl, combine the two flours with the salt. In another bowl or pitcher, beat the water with the yeast and honey. Mix the liquid into the dry ingredients, squeezing the dough through your fingertips until evenly but roughly combined. Cover and leave for 10 minutes.

Rub 1 tsp of corn or olive oil on the work-surface and knead the dough gently on the oiled surface for 10–15 seconds. Return the dough to the bowl, cover and leave for 10 minutes. Remove the dough from the bowl and knead once more on the oiled surface for 10–15 seconds. Place it back in the bowl, cover and leave for 10 minutes, then knead one final time for 10–15 seconds.

Give the dough a turn (see page 19), and repeat after 45 and 90 minutes.

By this time it should be puffy and the surface blistered with bubbles. On a well-floured surface, roll the dough out to a thickness of ½in. Using a 4in round cutter (I use a sharp edged plastic bowl), press down into the dough to create discs. Remove each disc and place them, spaced a few inches apart, on floured baking sheets. Cover with a cloth. Lightly re-knead the trimmings so that the dough is smooth again. Cover and leave for 10 minutes before rolling and cutting into the final discs. Leave the dough discs for 1½ hours, or until almost doubled in height.

Preheat the oven to 400°F. With floured fingertips, make dimples in the surface of each dough disc. Bake in the center of the oven for 25–30 minutes, or until the surface is gently browned. Slide the discs onto a cooling rack. If you prefer the breads softish, cover them with a cloth while they cool.

Salt crackers

These crisp, flaky, brittle flatbreads are made from a yeasty dough layered with a mixture of butter, flour, and baking soda. You need a soft flour to make the best crackers, so be on the lookout for flour milled from local varieties, which tend to be soft, as they will produce a cracker with a tender bite. Failing that, replace ¼ cup (25g) of the flour used in the dough with cornstarch or potato starch.

TIP One forgotten cracker, the Cumberland cream cracker, included caraway seeds in the mixture. This was typical of many crackers made at the start of the 20th century, such as Wiggs and the original Dr Abernethy's biscuit. Try seeding the top with either caraway, mustard, or dill seeds together with salt.

FOR THE ROLLING CRUMBS:
¼ cup (25g) all-purpose flour (100%)
½ tsp fine sea salt (1%)
½ tsp baking soda (1%)
2 tsp unsalted butter or good lard (40%)

FOR THE DOUGH:
½ tsp fresh yeast, crumbled (2%)
½ cup (125g) water at 68°F (62%)
1⅔ cups (200g) soft all-purpose flour (100%)
½ tsp fine sea salt (1%)
fine sea salt for dusting the crackers

FOR THE ROLLING CRUMBS In a bowl, combine the flour with the salt and baking soda. Blend the butter into the dry ingredients until the mixture resembles a fine crumble mix. Leave at room temperature while you prepare the other ingredients.

FOR THE DOUGH In a bowl or pitcher, beat the yeast with the water. In another bowl, combine the flour with the salt. Stir the dry ingredients into the liquid and combine the mixture into a dough.

Rub 1 tsp of corn or olive oil on the work-surface and knead the dough on the oiled surface for 10–15 seconds. Return it to the bowl, cover and leave for 15 minutes, then knead briefly once more. Place the dough back in the bowl, cover and leave for 2 hours, until it has almost doubled in size.

On a floured work-surface, roll the dough out into a ¼in-thick 12 x 8in rectangle, with the longest side facing you. Sprinkle the buttered flour rolling crumbs over two-thirds of the dough, then fold the remaining third back into the center. Fold the dough over once more so the crumbs are encased in the dough. Seal the edges of the dough, then roll it once more to measure 12 x 8in. Fold the dough in thirds again, then cover with a cloth and leave for 30 minutes.

Roll the dough out until it is a scant ¼in thick. Prick the surface of the dough with a fork. Cut squares from the dough, and place them on a baking sheet. I bake these a trayful at a time, rolling and cutting more as the previous ones bake.

Preheat the oven to 400°F. Lightly brush the top of the crackers with water and, using a tea-strainer and 1 tsp of salt, finely dust the top of the dough. Bake in the center of the oven for 30 minutes, or until the crackers are crisp, dry, and lightly browned on top. Transfer to a wire cooling rack, then bake the remaining dough.

Eat with slivers of good cheese or crumble roughly into something like a thick fish soup.

France

Long ago, many grand hotels contained their own bakeries. As with the old cruise ships, all of the cooking was carried out down in the depths, beneath the suites and rooms, by a vast coterie of talented chefs. Bread was rarely purchased already baked by these hotels. Dough would be mixed and baked through the night so that freshly made breads, made to perfected house recipes, were ready for every meal. These hotel kitchens were also training grounds for young apprentices—people who could learn a variety of skills from some of the finest craftsmen in their field. Few hotels operate in this way now; it has become more economical for them to buy in prepared ingredients, and sometimes meals, too. But in a few hotels, chefs continue to bake with a brilliant vigor.

It's night, and the bakers are at work in the basement of the Hôtel Plaza Athénée in Paris. The guests are asleep in their rooms upstairs when I arrive, just as the bakers are starting their shifts. Getting up at night for work is a strange task. The instinct is to stay very quiet, dodging the drunks and late-night party goers in order to weave a path to work. Night-bakers creep about in darkness, quietly turning keys and shutting doors, mumbling at bus drivers or taxi guys, only really awakening in the bright light of the noisy bakery and with the radiated warmth from the oven.

The Plaza Athénée is the Paris home of France's most revered contemporary chef de cuisine, Alain Ducasse. He is a talented, feisty maverick, who insists that the whole meal in his restaurant be extraordinary, and that the best bread be served with it. Since the restaurant is an asset to the hotel, the bakery is too, and is allowed to be excellent without too much hindrance from the money men. Nicolas Berger is the chef pâtissier for Alain Ducasse, and runs the pâtisserie and the bakery as part of his charge. Nicolas's work involves perfecting the recipes and keeping the output of each commis chef consistent, on time, and astounding.

I've come here on a pilgrimage to see a roll. It is a special, beautiful, spiky bread roll, with charred pointed ends and a bulbous middle that has been slashed twice with a blade. This is the most imitated roll that I know of, and replicas are seen in artisan bakeries around the world. The shape shows plainly that such rolls have not popped out of a machine as little dough balls. The tapered points can only be made by hand. They are fragile, baked in a

ABOVE, CLOCKWISE FROM TOP: Bakers working for Alain Ducasse; *petit pain* left to rise on a board; the Hôtel Plaza Athénée's lobby door, opulent with mirrors, gilding, and crystal. OPPOSITE, CLOCKWISE FROM TOP RIGHT: Head baker David Marquès; *petit epi*; the new classic dinner roll; freshly baked baguettes; David cuts the dough into a wheatsheaf shape; David rolling the pointed ends on the dinner roll; the rolls resting on a linen cloth. CENTER: a waiter places a roll on a restaurant table.

LEFT TO RIGHT: David Marquès carries the bread through the gleaming kitchen to the restaurant; David poses with his breads; a *couronne* cools upright in the bakery.

hot oven so that the edges are singed black, and possess a crust that is thin, golden, and crisp.

Because of the large number of rolls that the bakery makes, there is a machine to assist the combining of the dough. The flour, salt, water, and leavening are mixed very slowly in a machine called a petrin. The word "petrin" simply means mixer, but this type of mixer is a world away from the high-speed machines that have driven post-war baking. A pair of curved steel prongs gently flip the dough up and over, again and again, and the action of the dough rotates the bowl as it spins freely on a central pivot.

The petrin imitates the hand labor of a baker, gently stretching the dough with each rotation. There is nothing aggressive, energetic or aerobic here; just a quiet knead and a gentle pull. Leaven is added, but it is stored as dough rather than as a batter, and added only after the dough has been mixed and been left to rest. As the action of even this mixer is still more aggressive than that of the gentler hand, this delay in adding the leaven prevents over-stressing.

David Marquès is the young baker in charge of producing these rolls. All the bakers are immaculately groomed, with their crisp, white uniforms tied and tucked in closely. Twenty years ago in London, a young chef called Marco Pierre White worked in a uniform that looked like he'd been the victor of a food fight, and the sweat, grime, and disheveled appearance said "I am not a repressed robot but a vigorous chef who cares more about flavor than about personal appearance." But for one of him, a thousand others simply saw the grime as a masculine symbol, and today imitate the look rather than the effort and excellence that lay behind it. Here, David and the other bakers work clean and hard.

The dough for the rolls is shaped in stages. First, pieces of dough are weighed and pulled into small balls. This gives the baker an even shape to mold. After a short rest, the dough is rolled against a wooden surface. The heel of each hand stretches and rolls thin points on the ends of the rolls, and they are then left to rest on linen-covered trays. The long, shiny fibers in the linen stop the dough from sticking; cotton can leave woolly fibers in dough. Once the dough has risen slightly, David cuts the rolls with a sharp blade, then puts them straight into the oven at a high temperature. This causes the rolls to puff into buxom fullness, tearing along the cuts and charring on the tapered ends. They finally arrive on the lunch table looking perfect, and truly freshly baked.

I talk with Nicolas Berger in the comparative quiet after lunch service has finished. His admiration for Alain Ducasse is honest and quiet. "I know that it's pretty rare what we have here," he says. "It's because of Mr Ducasse that we're able to keep the quality of the bread."

Nicolas' father was a pastry chef, with a store in a little village. Nicolas continued his father's traditions, but after a while he became fascinated by bread, too. "Fifteen years ago it was pejorative to say, 'I'm a pastry chef who also bakes bread,' because the result was not that impressive then," he says. "But I don't agree with that at all today. Bread is so important for the whole meal, and it should be remarkable."

OATMEAL | **THE DRY BREADS OF WINTER**

Oatcakes

The gray-green colored oatcake, with its edges scorched ever so slightly in the oven, always has a place at my table. There is something about the dry, tender crumb that requires cheese or butter. Though we think of the oatcake as resolutely Scottish, when it is on a plate with cheddar, Roquefort, or Wensleydale, it becomes a bread with a universal, elemental flavor that does not distract from or taint the food served with it.

TIP Ideally, roll the dough out immediately, but if you can't you will find that the dough hardens. This isn't a problem; simply add a little more water to the dough and work this through with your fingertips until it is evenly combined, then roll it out.

1½ cups (250g) fine oatmeal (100%)
¾ tsp fine sea salt (1.5%)
½ tsp baking soda (0.5%)
1¼ tbsp (20g) unsalted butter or lard (8%)
6 tbsp (100g) water at 68°F (40%)
additional oatmeal for rolling

In a bowl, combine the oatmeal with the salt and baking soda. Blend the butter or lard through the dry ingredients until all of the lumps have disappeared. Add the water and mix until you have a soft dough.

Sprinkle a little fine oatmeal on the work-surface and place the dough on top of it. Sprinkle more oatmeal over the dough. Using the heel of your hand, bash the dough out to flatten it, then sprinkle more oatmeal on the top and underneath. Using a rolling pin, roll the dough to a scant ¼in thick. While doing this, constantly run a spatula underneath to make sure the dough isn't sticking to the work-surface. Cut out discs using a 3in cutter and put them onto a baking sheet.

Preheat the oven to 400°F. Bake in the center of the oven for 30–40 minutes, or until the oatcakes are tinged with brown around the circumference. Allow to cool on a wire rack.

Barley flatbread

FOR THE OVERNIGHT BATTER:
¾ cup (200g) boiling water (400%)
½ cup (50g) barley flour (100%)

FOR THE DOUGH:
the batter (166%)
1¼ cups (150g) barley flour (100%)
1 tsp ground barley malt (see malted grains on page 38–39) (3%)
½ tsp fresh yeast, crumbled (2%)
½ tsp fine sea salt (2%)
additional barley flour for dusting

These thin, brutal flat breads, with their strange, sweet barley-malt taste, would once have been a staple of a simple breakfast or supper, toasted and served hot and buttered alongside a cold bowl of buttermilk. The dough can be enriched with a little butter or lard to make a "fatty bread." In our affluent times, austere recipes serve as a reminder of simpler ways.

FOR THE OVERNIGHT BATTER Cool the water to 176°F, then, in a bowl, beat the barley flour into the water. Leave the mixture overnight, covered.

FOR THE DOUGH In a bowl, stir all the ingredients together until you have a soft dough. Scrape any remaining dough from your fingers into the bowl, cover, and leave in a warm place for 2 hours, or until the mixture has puffed up.

Lightly flour the work-surface and roll out the dough until it is about ¼in thick. Cut the dough into rectangles and place them on a baking sheet, with a gap of ½in between each one. Cover with a cloth and leave in a warm place for 45 minutes.

Preheat the oven to 410°F. Bake for 15 minutes, then reduce the heat to 350°F and bake for an additional 25 minutes, or until the barley breads are crisp and light. Cool on a wire rack and store in an airtight container.

BERRIES | THE DRY BREADS OF WINTER

Salty and sour berry crisp bread

1⅔ cups (200g) whole-wheat or spelt flour (66%)
¾ cup (100g) soft all-purpose flour (34%)
¼ tsp baking soda (0.5%)
¼ tsp baking powder (0.5%)
¼ tsp fine sea salt (0.5%)

2 tbsp unsalted butter, softened (10%)
3oz (80g) dried sweetened berries, chopped (27%)
½ cup (125g) water at 68°F (42%)
1 tsp powdered dried cloudberries or ground sumac or lemon zest
salt flakes for sprinkling

Johan Sörbergs, a remarkable young Swedish baker in Stockholm, makes very thin rye crisp breads dusted ever so lightly with a ground powder made from the local yellow cloudberry, which has an acid-fruity sharpness and a sulfurous color that stains the top of the bread. I've combined this idea with putting berries in the bread, so doubling the flavor. Since it is hard to find cloudberries outside Scandinavia, other dried sharp berries can be used. Red currants, gooseberries, or cranberries, though usually sweetened with sugar before drying, are suitable. Yet this sweetness loses the fruit's zing. A better replacement is the ground sumac spice found in Lebanese food stores. As a last resort, use grated lemon zest.

In a bowl, combine the two flours with the baking soda, baking powder, and salt. Blend the softened butter into these dry ingredients until it is evenly incorporated and the mixture slightly resembles very fine bread crumbs. Stir in the chopped berries, then add the water. Scrunch the dough together with your fingers so that it is evenly mixed.

Preheat the oven to 425°F. Lightly dust the work-surface with flour. Cut the dough in half, and keep one half in the bowl covered with a cloth while you roll out the other. While you roll, keep checking that the dough isn't sticking to the work-surface, but use only a little flour to achieve this. Roll out the dough until it is about ⅛in thick, then prick the surface all over with a fork. Use a sharp knife or pastry wheel to cut squares in the dough, roughly 4in across. Brush the surface with a little water, then sprinkle on the powdered cloudberries (or sumac or lemon zest).

Transfer these squares to a baking sheet lined with non-stick parchment paper, then sprinkle a few flakes of sea salt on the top of each. Bake for 10–12 minutes, until the breads are slightly puffed and tinged dark brown at the edges. While the breads are baking, roll out and finish the remaining dough.

Transfer the breads to a wire rack to cool. Store in an airtight container.

Scotland

Bread-making is unlikely to involve invention, but it must depend on rediscovery. As part of this, bringing back old grains helps millers and farmers to practice traditional production methods by placing them in context. Traditional mills grind hard grains into flour in much the same way as they have for hundreds of years. The millstones that were used by our grandparents look much like the millstones that we use now in restored water or windmills. The grain may even make flour that tastes the same as it did then, though we will never really know that for sure.

Bere is a type of barley that was once widely cultivated for food in Scotland, Ireland, and parts of northern Europe. Though bere may have existed in Scotland since Neolithic times, it was probably introduced as a crop by the Vikings between 787 and 950. The name could have derived from the old Icelandic "barr," a type of local barley that was once cultivated there.

Bere is the root of other words in our language. The word "barn" means "barley place," and stems from a combination of barley (bere) and house (aern). The word beer was spelt "bere" during the Jacobean period, and previously by the Anglo-Saxons as "beor"; in Britain, beer is brewed by steeping sprouted and toasted barley grains in warm water that has been mixed with an infusion of hops, and then fermenting this concoction with yeast.

Together with oats, bere once formed an important part of the diet of Highland people, as both of these grains would grow in difficult Highland soils and ripen during a short growing season. Much like rye, bere did not bind into an elastic loaf that is capable of trapping air to make it light and crisp. Instead, it would be mixed into a batter, or patted out flat between the hands, and tossed on to a hot "girdle" to make a thin round loaf called a bannock. Oatcakes are made in a similar way, using oats.

It was difficult to keep the grain dry, though communities would dry it in a local "corn" kiln (corn was a term applied to all grain). With dampness, some grain would inevitably sprout, resulting in an unintentional malting, and sweetening, of the final flour. At home, bere would be scorched in a kettle over the fire to make it hard enough to grind.

Golspie Mill, a one-and-a-quarter-hour drive north of Inverness, is one place where bere and peasemeal (a flour made from yellow peas) are still kilned and milled traditionally. Michael Shaw spends a hectic few hours

ABOVE, CLOCKWISE FROM TOP: The release plug that allows the water to run down the mill laide; the hole where the grain enters the millstone; Munlochy Bay, opposite Donnie MacLeod's farm; the mill wall covered in vine tendrils. OPPOSITE, CLOCKWISE FROM TOP LEFT: across the mill pond at Golspie Mill; miller Michael Shaw standing in the kiln used to toast the bere meal; sacks of rye grain on the upper floor of the mill; the geese and the mill wheel; the wooden framework around the millstone; a wheatmeal, bere, and oat loaf, stacked by the trout pond; Donnie MacLeod's dog, Bess. CENTER: Michael and Becky Shaw.

> "When people talk about our national health insurance, that 'insurance' is in our soil. The seeds, grains, plants, and the wildlife that depends on them, must be kept protected from harm."
> DONNIE MACLEOD

LEFT TO RIGHT: a Prunus in blossom; farmer and activist Donnie MacLeod, of MacLeod Organics in Ardersier, on the Black Isle.

each morning running up and down the wooden stairs in a setting that resembles a bleached-wood Meccano set, making sure that the cogs turn, the sacks are lifted, and the stones rotate. His working hours are compressed because the source of power to turn the wheel—the water—is limited.

A small burn fills a mill pond approximately 30 yards across. This takes about a day to fill, though less time in the rainy seasons, when excess water overflows through the trout pond. To work the mill, a large plug on a chain is opened and the water runs down a narrow mill laide (race) to turn the wheel. A full mill pond gives about two hours of power, and during that time it is necessary to make the most of the energy that is provided by the turning wheel. Other than grinding the grains, the water powers various sieves, a fanner to blow the dust and husk off the grain, and a rope hoist to move the sacks of grain and flour between the floors.

I sat with Michael and his partner Becky around the old Aga in the miller's house. "I arrived from New Zealand and worked the first season as a shearer," said Michael. "Milling isn't something that, as a child, you'd think you would grow up and want to do, is it? It never even occurred to me that there would be such a thing happening."

The previous miller, Fergus, and his wife were retiring and they needed someone to take over. "Fergus showed me the mill and I thought: 'Wow, check this out!'" says Michael. "It had that grainy sort of smell. The bere was moving through my hands, cogs were turning, and belts were moving, and I thought: 'Oh yeah, this might be something to have a look at.' Other people were interested but we got selected over the, er, rivals."

Becky adds, laughing: "Fergus said that the others were from somewhere in England, and all they wanted to talk about was 'the money,' and he straightaway didn't like them."

Every so often, Michael takes a delivery of his flours to MacLeod Organics in Ardersier, the home and base of the farmer and activist Donnie MacLeod. The village sits on the shore of the Moray Firth, and is so close to the sea that you can feel the salt drying your skin, and the sea air cleansing your eyes and breath. Early in 2002, Donnie was arrested for failing to cooperate after refusing to move from a GM crop trial, and the subsequent press support turned him into a local hero. For now, the trial is on hold.

We take a ride out on his tractor around the paddocks, as he feeds his cows organic carrots dug from his fields. "The cows really love carrots," he says, as they rush around the back of the trailer that tips piles of orange roots onto the green grass and clover.

MacLeod Organics delivers boxes of organic vegetables and ingredients to customers in the area, and among the onions, potatoes, and seasonal vegetables, Golspie Mill's packets of oatmeal, whole-wheat flour, beremeal, and peasemeal can also be ordered. One of Donnie's customers is a local family on a low income who bake at home; in return for an organic box they help around the farm with bits of weeding.

"When people talk about our national health insurance, that 'insurance' is in our soil," says Donnie. "The seeds, grains, plants, and the wildlife that depends on them must be kept protected from chemical harm. It is that pure food our children must be allowed to eat, and I will fight for that to be."

Anchovy buttons

These small crackers, each with a nugget of butter-cooked anchovy nestling in the center, are good to serve with a glass of cold beer. Beef dripping makes the taste of breads like this more full and rich than their ingredients might suggest.

TIP This recipe is open to variations according to what you have or like to eat. You could use butter or good pork lard instead of beef dripping. If millet is difficult to find, then cornmeal or ground rice could be substituted.

2 cups (250g) soft all-purpose flour (83%)
2oz (50g) finely ground millet (17%)
½ tsp baking soda (1%)
½ tsp fine sea salt (1%)
⅓ cup (75g) beef dripping (25%)
6 tbsp (90g) water at 68°F (30%)

FOR THE ANCHOVY BUTTER:
1 tbsp unsalted butter
3–4 good anchovies, finely chopped
a sliver of garlic

In a bowl, combine the flour, millet, soda, and salt. Using your fingers, work the dripping into the dry ingredients until the mixture resembles coarse bread crumbs. Slowly add the water, and work it in until you have a soft, smooth dough.

Lightly flour the work-surface and roll the dough to a scant ¼in thick. Using a ½in round cutter, cut discs from the dough and lift them with a knife onto a parchment-lined baking sheet.

Preheat the oven to 400°F. Place the anchovies, butter, and garlic in a small saucepan and heat until the butter melts and the mixture begins to sizzle. Remove from the heat and allow to cool a little, then, using a pastry brush or a teaspoon, spread a little anchovy butter over the surface of each cracker. The idea is to lightly coat the surface so it flavors the biscuit without running down the sides. Finally, dot a small piece of anchovy in the center of each biscuit.

Bake in the center of the oven for 20 minutes, or until the crackers have just started to brown. Remove from the sheet and cool on a wire rack. When cold, store in an airtight container.

Rosemary and fresh cheese sticks

Salty food, served late in the afternoon, brings on a thirst and provides an excuse to drink a cocktail or *apéritif*. These slivers of dough, made from a mixture flavored and moistened with soft fresh cheese and the oily herb rosemary, are generously salted. In Italy, there are many versions of what they call *grissini*, sometimes plain, sometimes light and open-textured. At Giorgio Locatelli's restaurant in London, *grissini* are tipped with a shaving of the best ham from Parma, making them perfect to sit in a flute on a table, to be served with a glass of dry Prosecco or sparkling water.

TIP Other herbs can be used to flavor this bread. Try adding the following to the dough: lemon thyme, marjoram, sage, or chives, cut fine.

FOR THE FERMENT:

1¼ cups (150g) soft all-purpose flour (100%)

1 cup (250g) whole milk (166%)

¾ tsp fresh yeast, crumbled (3%)

FOR THE DOUGH:

2 cups (250g) soft all-purpose flour (100%)

1 tsp fine sea salt (2%)

⅓ cup (80g) unsalted butter (32%)

¼ cup (50g) fresh curd cheese, such as ricotta (20%)

large sprig of rosemary, chopped (2%)

the ferment (162%)

FOR THE FERMENT In a bowl, combine all the ingredients and leave in a warm place for 1 hour.

FOR THE DOUGH In a bowl, combine the flour with the salt. Blend the butter, cheese, and rosemary into the dry ingredients until the butter and cheese are evenly mixed. This blending will help the rosemary release its aromatic oil into the flour.

Stir the ferment into the flour mixture, and scrunch the dough together with your hands until evenly mixed. Scrape any remaining dough from your fingers into the bowl, cover and leave for 10 minutes.

Rub 1 tsp of corn or olive oil on the work-surface and knead the dough on the oiled surface for 10 seconds, ending with a smooth, round ball. Wipe the bowl clean, replace the dough, cover and leave for an additional 10 minutes. Repeat this light kneading twice more at 10-minute intervals. Then leave the dough for 1 hour, kneading it once more during that time.

Preheat the oven to 350°F. Lightly flour the work-surface and roll the dough out into an 8 x 12in rectangle. Cut thin strips across the width of the dough, each less than ½in thick, then roll these with your hands on the work-surface so they elongate and become strands of dough about 16in long. Lay them on a baking sheet lined with non-stick parchment paper, leaving a little space in-between so they do not stick together when they expand in the oven.

Bake in the center of the oven for 25–30 minutes, or until the sticks are crisp and golden brown. With my oven, it helps to flip the sticks over three-quarters of the way through the cooking so that they get evenly browned. Remove the sticks from the sheet and allow to cool on a wire rack while you bake the remainder.

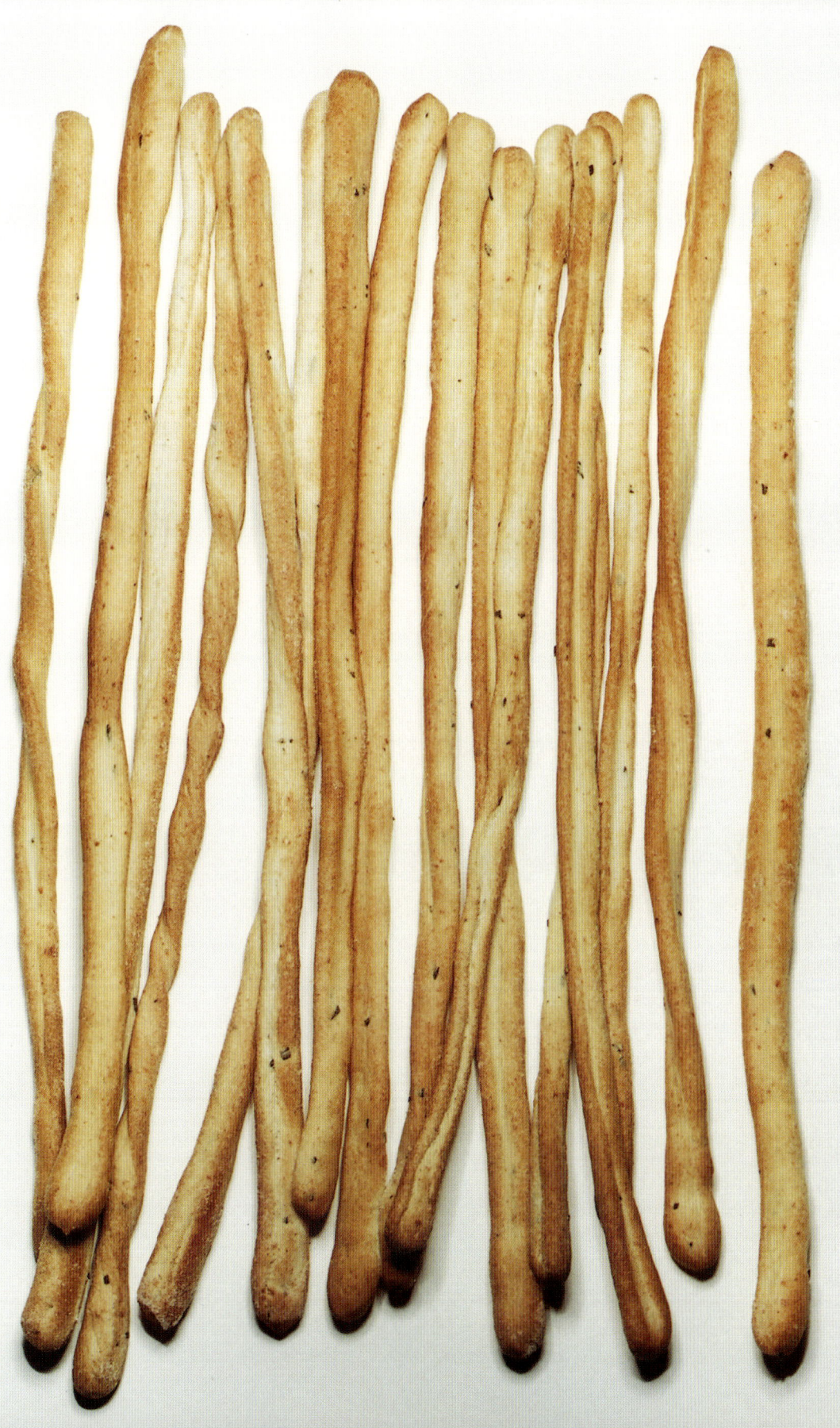

White bean wafer

This thin crisp bread uses that old standby for the humble loaf, the bean. When there was insufficient flour to make a loaf, or where the local flour was coarse and unappetizing, the addition of either cooked beans or rice added bulk to the dough and softened the taste. Now we know it would have also increased the nutritional content of the bread, making it higher in protein and good for a diet with little meat or fish. Serve with a fresh tomato salad, good when the new season's tomatoes are ripe and peppery from the vine, and a few soft olives.

TIP Try other cooked legumes, such as chickpeas or cranberry beans, and combine them with herbs or paprika.

1 cup (200g) cooked white beans, drained well and dried on kitchen towel (100%)

1½ cups (200g) soft all-purpose flour (100%)

½ tsp baking soda (1%)

½ tsp baking powder (1%)

¾ tsp fine sea salt (1.5%)

¼ cup (50g) unsalted butter (25%)

2 tbsp (30g) water at 68°F (15%)

sea salt flakes

Using a mortar and pestle, or a food processor, mash the beans until you have a fine, smooth paste. In a bowl, combine the flour, soda, baking powder, and salt. Blend the butter into these dry ingredients, then add the bean paste and water, working them in well with your fingers until you have a soft, smooth dough.

Preheat the oven to 400°F. Roll out the dough on a floured work-surface until it is a scant ¼in thick. Cut the dough into rectangles measuring 2 x 4in, and place these on a baking sheet lined with non-stick parchment. Brush a little water down the center of each wafer, and sprinkle a line of sea salt flakes down the middle of each.

Bake in the center of the oven for 15–20 minutes, or until the wafers are lightly brown at the edges. Transfer to a wire rack and leave in a warm place so that they continue to dry and become crisp. When cold, store in an airtight container.

The finish

Often, prior to baking, I leave a loaf crusted in the flour that protected the dough from the cloth. But an extra dusting of coarse semolina or whole-wheat flour, or a light brush with olive oil, can elevate the crust. These recipes will help you perfect that special finish.

Custard for baking

1¾ cups (400g) fresh milk
1 vanilla bean, split and seeds scraped out
3 tbsp cornstarch
½ cup (125g) superfine sugar
2 medium eggs
¼ cup (50g) unsalted butter, softened

In a saucepan, heat the milk with the vanilla bean and its seeds and scrapings until hot and nearly boiling. Remove from the heat and allow to infuse for 5 minutes. Remove the bean.

In a bowl, mix the cornstarch with the sugar. Beat in the eggs, one at a time, until smooth and combined. Beat the hot milk into the mixture, return to the saucepan, and heat, beating constantly, until it comes to a boil. Remove from the heat, transfer immediately into a cooler container, and beat in the softened butter.

Press a piece of buttered paper (or the butter wrapper) onto the surface of the custard and then allow to cool.

Starch glaze

The brilliantine of loaf finishes, this starch glaze gives a polished appearance to the loaf and was much used at the beginning of the 20th century. Simply a boiled mixture of starch and water, it sets quickly in the oven and creates a smooth varnish that gives the loaf a satin sheen after baking.

6 tbsp cornstarch or potato starch
¾ cup (200g) water

Mix the cornstarch with a few tablespoons of the water to soften it, then beat in the remaining water. Place this mixture in a saucepan and bring to a boil, stirring constantly. Remove from the heat and allow to cool.

To use, brush the loaf with the glaze about 15 minutes before the end of baking.

Egg glaze

It was in the Ukraine where I first saw a baker tie together a few long chicken feathers to make a simple brush. The brush was then dipped into a cup which contained a fresh egg beaten into a vivid orange wash for the top of the loaf (see above). The chickens, fed on the crusts of bread, beetles, and corncobs, and the enrichment of both the crust and crumb of the loaf by the eggs, gave a strong sense of their place in that family's nourishment.

Bakers have different preferences when brushing the unbaked loaf with egg. Some prefer just the yolks, mixed with the same weight of cold water and a pinch of salt. This gives a very strongly colored wash that darkens quickly in the oven and retains the mark of the brush when baked. Others use the whole egg, beaten—sometimes with a little milk—which will give a gentle, golden sheen to the baked loaf. Usually the flavor of the egg remains, so make sure it's fresh, and don't leave the wash sitting around for too long before using it, as it can soon develop an "off" aroma.

Salt-water wash

This will give a salty crust to small rolls or a large loaf and is best used in combination with a reduction in the amount of salt in the dough.

6 tbsp (100g) boiling water
3 tbsp fine sea salt

Pour the boiling water over the salt, and stir until the salt has dissolved. Apply with a pastry brush just before baking.

Boiled sugar glaze

The sticky sweet glaze of a boiled syrup is often part of the appeal of sweet buttery breads. It is drenched on after baking but, once the bread is cold, it stays glossy and sticks to everything the loaf touches. If you brush it on while the loaf is still hot, it tends to crystallize and dry white and mat.

150g superfine sugar
6 tbsp (100g) water

Warm the sugar and water together in a saucepan, stirring until the sugar has dissolved. Bring the syrup to a boil and simmer for 2 minutes. Remove from the heat and leave undisturbed to cool.

Dusting with powdered or superfine sugar

Some breads can be dusted with powdered or superfine sugar just before baking, particularly those enriched breads that are baked for a short time. Don't think this is simply for sweet breads, however; the salty cracker dusted in sugar is an odd but good chew. Place either sugar in a tea-strainer or sieve, on a plate. Then carefully lift the strainer over the bread and gently dredge the sugar over the top of the loaf, roll, or cracker.

Coarse-grain or seed crust

Flaked wheat, rolled oats, or seeds are good on the outside of a loaf. The way to stick them on is to roll the unbaked loaf on a wet cloth lying on a tray, then in one swift move roll the loaf again on a tray covered with your chosen grain or seed. This light coating of water makes the grain or seed stick, and gives a very smart cloak to the crust of the loaf.

Alcohol wash

Sometimes dough is brushed with alcohol before baking to stick sugar, say, to the crust so that only its underlying flavor remains and the alcohol evaporates in the oven. Other times it is brushed or poured onto the loaf after baking. At Maison Bertaux, an old Anglo-French pastry shop in London's Soho district, they keep a bottle of rum by the cash till for dousing each baba as it is sold. Lovely.

Butter-crumb crust

Bread crumbs can be used as a crust on a loaf in the same way as grains and seeds. Flavorings, such as garlic, anchovy, ground black pepper, or paprika can be added to the crumbs.

5 cups (250g) coarse or fine bread crumbs
¼ cup (50g) melted butter
½ tsp fine sea salt

Place the bread crumbs in a bowl and pour the melted butter over them. Stir, add the salt, then rub the crumbs in your hands to make sure the butter and salt are evenly combined. Spread these out on a tray and then, as with the grain method, roll the unbaked loaf on a wet cloth before rolling it in the buttered crumbs.

WEIGHT	
metric	imperial
5g	⅛oz
10g	¼oz
15g	½oz
25-30g	1oz
35g	1¼oz
40g	1½oz
50g	1¾oz
55g	2oz
60g	2¼oz
70g	2½oz
85g	3oz
90g	3¼oz
100g	3½oz
115g	4oz
125g	4½oz
140g	5oz
150g	5½oz
175g	6oz
200g	7oz
225g	8oz
250g	9oz
275g	9¾oz
280g	10oz
300g	10½oz
325g	11½oz
350g	12oz
375g	13oz
400g	14oz
425g	15oz
450g	1lb
500g	1lb 2oz
550g	1lb 4oz
600g	1lb 5oz
650g	1lb 7oz
700g	1lb 9oz
750g	1lb 10oz
800g	1lb 12oz
850g	1lb 14oz
900g	2lb
950g	2lb 2oz
1kg	2lb 4oz
1.25kg	2lb 12oz
1.3kg	3lb
1.5kg	3lb 5oz
1.6kg	3lb 8oz
1.8kg	4lb
2kg	4lb 8oz
2.25kg	5lb
2.5kg	5lb 8oz
2.7kg	6lb
3kg	6lb 8oz

VOLUME		
metric	imperial	
1.25ml	¼ teaspoon	
2.5ml	½ teaspoon	
5ml	1 teaspoon	
10ml	2 teaspoons	
15ml	1 tablespoon	
30ml	1 fl oz	
50ml	2 fl oz	¼ cup
75ml	2½ fl oz	
100ml	3½ fl oz	
125ml	4 fl oz	½ cup
150ml	5 fl oz	
175ml	6 fl oz	¾ cup
200 ml	7 fl oz	
225 ml	8 fl oz	1 cup
250ml	9 fl oz	
300ml	10 fl oz	
350ml	12 fl oz	
400ml	14 fl oz	
425ml	15 fl oz	
450ml	16 fl oz	2 cups
500ml	18 fl oz	
600ml	20 fl oz	
700ml	1¼ pints	
850ml	1½ pints	
1 litre	1¾ pints	4 cups
1.2 litres	2 pints	
1.3 litres	2¼ pints	
1.4 litres	2½ pints	
1.5 litres	2¾ pints	
1.7 litres	3 pints	

These charts are reproduced with the kind permission of The Guild of Food Writers.

Author's acknowledgments

To my editor Rebecca Spry, for her patience, and to Yasia Williams, Lawrence Morton, and Hattie Ellis, thanks for working so hard and taking the effort to make it good; my friends Dean Brettschneider, Richard Whittington, and Richard Bertinet for their encouragement and humor through it all; Giorgio and Plaxi Locatelli, Federico Turri, Federico Sali, and the staff at Locanda Locatelli; Susan Low and Guy Dimond; Wendy Fogarty; Patricia and Paul Harrison at Ceci Paolo, Ledbury, www.cecipaolo.com; Marie and Nick Daffern and their family at Hope End, www.hopeend.com; Troels Bendix, www.breadsetcetera.com; Sylvia Macdonald and Garry Parker at the British Baker; Chris Smail, Karen Tilley, Neville Moon, Rachel Saunders, and the staff at Bakehouse; Judy and David Horgan, Adrian Watson, Murray Rhind, and the bakers at Café Royal, Newcastle; Sharron, Tamara, and Evelyn at Snappy Snaps, Tooting; Colin Bradbury and the staff at Genie Imaging, www.genieimaging.co.uk; Clive Mellum and John Lister at Shipton Mill; and Alastair Hendy for putting me in a good light.

FOR HELP WITH THE SCIENCE: Ian Roberts, Chris Bond, and the staff at the National Collection of Yeast Cultures, Norwich, www.ncyc.co.uk; Professor Peter Shewry from Rothamsted Research, Harpenden, www.rothamsted.bbsrc.ac.uk; Dr. James Barnett; Keith Wooller at ADM Milling.

TO THE FOLLOWING BAKERS, MILLERS, FARMERS, AND FAMILIES:
SWEDEN: Dag Hermelin, Lisa Förare Winbladh, Johan Sörbergs at Riddarbageriet, Stockholm; Robert Saberski at Roslagsbröd, Gimo, www.roslagsbrod.se; Jan Hedh, Olof Viktors, Glemmingebro, www.olofviktors.se; Östen Brolin, Vete-Katten, Stockholm, www.vetekatten.se;
DENMARK: Camilla Plum and Per Koelster, Fuglebjerggaard, Helsinge, www.fuglebjerggaard.dk;
FRANCE: Nicolas Berger and his staff, Hélène Barbier and Emmanuelle Perrier, for Alain Ducasse, Hôtel Plaza Athénée, www.plaza-athenee-paris.com;
IRELAND: Michael Power and Ann Sutton, The Bakehouse, New Ross, Co. Wexford; Will Sutherland and Angela Ashe, School for Self Sufficiency; Killowen, New Ross, Co. Wexford, www.self-sufficiency.net;
SCOTLAND: Mike and Becky Shaw, Golspie Mill, Sutherland, www.golspiemill.co.uk; Donnie MacLeod, MacLeod Organics, Ardersier, Inverness, www.macleodorganics.com;
GERMANY: Isa Petereit, Julia Decker, Franz Stricker, Klenstrasse 69, Munich;
RUSSIA: Lilia Smelkolva at Slow Food, Bra, Italy; Ekaterina Drozdova; William Webster; Sofia Shurovskaia; Jonathan Thatcher;
UKRAINE: Paul Okopsky and Ukrainian Travel, www.Ukraine.co.uk; Mrs Yaroslava Kharuk and her son Andre, and the staff at Manchester Café, Ivano-Frankivsk; Oxana Yefimchuk; Igor Aveolyan; Mother Theresa and the Congregation of Sisters Meronocyts, Ivano-Frankivsk;
ITALY: Toni Vitiello, Claudio, Stella at Focacceria Tipica Ligure, Torino; Silvia Capello; Marta Bera at Panetteria Bera; the staff at Latteria Bera Bruna;
ENGLAND: Jack and Jill Lang; Andy Lynes at www.egullet.com; Jim Webb, Yotam, Noam, and the staff at Ottolenghi; Michael Stoate, Cann Mills, Dorset; Aiden Chapman and the staff at Leakers bakery; Emmanuel Hadjiandreou at Daylesford Farm, Gloucestershire.

INDEX

A
alcohol wash 188
ale bread with wheat grains 48
almond-milk loaf 118
almonds, orange and almond cake 131
Alsace loaf with rye 49
anchovy buttons 181
apples
    layered apple and custard loaf 120
    rolled oat and apple bread 82
Armagnac syrup 104

B
babas, prune and rye babas with Armagnac syrup 104
bakers' percentages 12
baking the loaf 22
baking stones 22
ball, shaping a 21
barley
    barley bread 77
    barley flatbread 176
    barley flour 36, 77, 132, 176
    barley and ryebread 36
    lemon barley cob 132
barm 38, 40
    barm bread 41
    fruited barm cake 103
baton, shaping a 21
bay leaves, onion and bay loaf 116
beans, white bean wafer 184
beer
    ale bread with wheat grains 48
    for barm-making 40, 41
bere 86
black currants, sweet black currant crown 115
black pepper pancakes 123
buckwheat
    griddled buckwheat muffins 96
    pancakes 78
buns
    Chelsea buns 128
    flaky butter buns 146
    sweet brandy buns 58
butter
    brown butter picklets 156
    butter-crumb crust 188
    flaky butter buns 146
    sweet butter dough 145
buttermilk, barley flatbread 176
    Waterford soda bread 69

C
caraway, light caraway rye 68
cassis and currant loaf 60
cheese
    rosemary and fresh cheese sticks 182
    sage, cheese, and shallot pie 154
    used as ingredient 152
Chelsea buns 128
cherry, fennel, and rye loaf 106
chestnuts
    sweet chestnut and hazelnut bread 114
    white loaf with grated chestnuts 163
chickpea pancakes 153
cider 53
cinnamon, raisin and cinnamon loaf 100
cobnut loaf with honey and grains 112
confectioners' custard, *see* custard for baking; pastry custard
coriander, in rye bread 130
corn flour
    corn bread 73
    mustard and corn rolls 139
    white corn and wheat bread 35
    see also cornmeal
cornmeal
    crisp cornmeal sticks 74
    see also corn flour
crisp breads
    crisp cornmeal sticks 74
    dark crisp rye bread 167
    salt crackers 171
    salty and sour berry crisp bread 177
crust finishes 57, 187–88, 188
crusty potato bread 42
cucumber pickle juice 57
curds 44, 45
    soft curd loaf 152
currants
    cassis and currant loaf 60
    Chelsea buns 128
    spotted soda bread 99
    soft curd loaf 152
    sweet saffron bread 124
custard for baking 187

D
dark crisp rye bread 167
Denmark, bread-makers 70–72
dill
    dill pickle rye 57
    fried flatbread with dill seeds and pork crackling 164
dough
    mixing 18–19
    shaping 20–21
    slashing 22
    sweet butter dough 145
    turning 19
dumplings, garlic dumplings 142
dusting, with powdered or superfine sugar 188

E
egg glaze 187
England, bread-makers 160–62
equipment 22
    Pullman loaf pan 89, 118

F
fat 144
fennel seeds, cherry, fennel, and rye loaf 106
figs, in red wine loaf 54
finishing 187–88
five-grain loaf 81
flaky butter buns 146
flatbreads
    barley flatbread 176
    dark crisp rye bread 167
    fried, with dill seeds and pork crackling 164
    light rye flatbread 168
    oatcakes 175
    olive oil flatbread 151
    sage, cheese, and shallot pie 154
    salty and sour berry crisp bread 177
    white potato stottie cake 119
flax seed *see* linseed
flour 13
flours, for making leaven 25
France, bread-makers 172–74
fried flatbread with dill seeds and pork crackling 164
fromage frais, making curds 45
fruited barm cake 103
fruited breads 60, 82, 99, 100, 103, 104, 106, 115

G
garlic
    dumplings 142
    garlic and goose fat pancakes 157
Germany, bread-makers 90–92
ginger, honey and ginger wafers 140
glazes 187, 188
gluten 14, 36, 64
golden raisins, *used as ingredient* 99, 103
Golspie loaf 86
goose fat, garlic and goose fat pancakes 157
grains
    coarse grain or seed crust 188
    cooked or soaked 48, 49, 64, 77, 81, 115
    malted 38
    sprouted 38–39
griddles 96

H
hazelnuts, sweet chestnut and hazelnut bread 114 *see also* cobnut
herbs, *used as ingredient* 57, 127, 130, 135, 153, 154, 182
honey
    cobnut loaf with honey and grains 112
    honey and ginger wafers 140
    whey bread with butter and honey 45
hops, bitter hops 38

I/K
Ireland, bread-makers 108–10
Italian "00" flour 35, 150
Italy, bread-makers 148–50
kneading dough 18–19

L
lard cake 158

INDEX

layered apple and custard loaf 120
leaven
    barm 38, 40–41
    creating a leaven 24
    recipe 25–27, 31
    storage 27
    see also yeast
leaven breads
    ale bread with wheat grains 48
    barley and rye 36
    crusty potato bread 42
    mill loaf 30
    sour 100% rye bread 31
    white 28
    white corn and wheat 35
lemon barley cob 132
lentil rolls 88
light caraway rye bread 68
light rye flatbread 168
linseed, linseed and wheat bread 94
liquids, for bread-making 44

M/N

malt 16
malted grains 38, 39
malting, home-malting 39
maltose 38
milk
    milk loaf 46
    sour milk 68
mill loaf 30
millet 63, 81, 93, 181
moist environment, importance of 22
Moscow, bread-makers 32–34
muffins, griddled buckwheat 96
Munich, bread-makers 90–92
mustard and corn rolls 139
nuts, breads using 54, 111–14, 118, 131

O

oatcakes 175
oatmeal, Golspie loaf 86
oats, rolled oat and apple bread 82
oiled surfaces 18, 19, 21
olive oil flatbread 151
olives, in white thyme bread 135
onions, onion and bay loaf 116
orange and almond cake 131
oven thermometer 22, 39
ovens 22

P/Q

pancakes
    black pepper 123
    brown butter picklets 156
    buckwheat 78
    chickpea 153
    farinata 153
    garlic and goose fat 157
pans, Pullman loaf pan 89, 118
Paris, bread-makers 172–74
parsley potato cakes 127
pastry custard, layered apple and custard loaf 120
peel (semolina dusted board) 22
percentages 12
picklets, brown butter picklets 156
pine nuts, in red wine loaf 54
pizza shovel 22
polenta, in corn bread 73
polished crust 57
pork crackling, fried flatbread with dill seeds and 164
potatoes
    parsley potato cakes 127
    crusty potato bread 42
    white potato stottie cake 119
prunes, prune and rye babas with Armagnac syrup 104
Pullman loaf pan 89, 118
Quick white loaf 63

R

raisins, raisin and cinnamon loaf 100
red wine loaf with pine nuts and figs 54
rennet 45
rice bread 89
rolled oat and apple bread 82
rolls
    lentil rolls 88
    mustard and corn rolls 139
rosemary and fresh cheese sticks 182
Russia, bread-makers 32–34
rye bread
    100% sour 31
    Alsace loaf with rye 49
    barley and ryebread 36
    cherry, fennel, and rye loaf 106
    with coriander 130
    dark crisp rye bread 167
    dill pickle rye 57
    light caraway rye 68
    light rye flatbread 168
    sweet rye 66
    wholegrain 85
rye flour 25, 30, 31, 36, 48, 66
    in prune and rye babas with Armagnac syrup 104
rye mix, gelatinized 31

S

saffron, sweet saffron bread 124
sage, cheese, and shallot pie 154
salt 16, 18
salt crackers 171
salt-water wash 188
salty and sour berry crisp bread 177
Scotland, bread-makers 178–80
scrumpy 53
scrumpy buns 53
sea salt 188
shallots
    sage, cheese, and shallot pie 154
simple milk loaf 46
slashing the dough 22
soda bread
    spotted soda bread 99
    Waterford soda bread 69
soft curd loaf 152
sour 100% rye bread 31
sourdough bread 24
spices, *used as ingredient* 66, 68, 100, 106, 123, 124, 128–30, 139–40
sprouted grains 38, 39
starch glaze 187
sticks
    crisp cornmeal sticks 74
    rosemary and fresh cheese sticks 182
    shaping 21
stottie cake, white potato stottie cake 119
sugar, for dusting bread 188
sunflower seeds, sunflower bread 93
Sweden, bread-makers 136
sweet black currant crown 115
sweet brandy buns 58
sweet butter dough 145
sweet chestnut and hazelnut bread 114
sweet rye bread 66
sweet saffron bread 124
syrup, corn or maple 46

T/U

thyme, white thyme bread 135
Turin, bread-makers 148–50
Ukraine, bread-makers 50–52

V/W

vinschgauer schüttelbrot 91, 92
wafers
    honey and ginger wafers 140
    white bean wafer 184
    see also biscuits
walnut bread 111
Waterford soda bread 69
weights and measurements 12
wheatgerm bread 64
whey 35, 44, 45
    whey bread with butter and honey 45
wholegrain rye bread 85
white bean wafer 184
white flour
    bread flour 25, 36
white leaven bread 28
white loaf with grated chestnuts 163
white corn and wheat loaf 35
white potato stottie cake 119
white thyme bread 135
whole-wheat flour 30, 35, 64
wine
    Alsace (white wine) loaf with rye 49
    red wine loaf with pine nuts and figs 54
work-surfaces, oiled 18, 19, 21

Y

yeast 15 *see also* leaven
yeasted butter dough 115, 120, 145
yogurt, low-fat 25